NEW MEXICO'S

LOST WORLDS & ENCHANTED LANDS

Three Rivers petroglyph site. (author's photo)

NEW MEXICO'S
LOST WORLDS & ENCHANTED LANDS

John LeMay

DEAD HORSE HISTORY

A SUBSIDIARY OF BICEP BOOKS. ROSWELL, NEW MEXICO

Printed in the United States of America

LeMay, John.
New Mexico's Lost Worlds & Enchanted Lands
ISBN 978-1-953221-18-6
New Mexico—Archeology/Folklore

For Bronco Sue
(Donna Blake Birchell's Ford, not the Old West serial killer)

Conquistador by Frederick Remington, 1889.

A NOTE FROM THE AUTHOR

"For God! For gold! For glory!"—motto of the Spanish Conquistador

In addition to being the Land of Enchantment, New Mexico is also a land of lost worlds. And, as a kid, I loved stories of lost worlds. Some of the better examples included Edgar Rice Burroughs' books like *The Land That Time Forgot* and its better-known precursor, *The Lost World*, by Sir Arthur Conan Doyle. Then there were movies like 1958's *The 7th Voyage of Sinbad*, featuring a lost land populated by ancient ruins, magicians, and mythical creatures animated by Ray Harryhausen. I was seven years old when I saw the film, and little did I know that my home state of New Mexico harbored some equally fantastic legends.

For instance, if you were told of a city ruled by a mythical king who flew away on a giant eagle, and who also left behind an immortality-granting flame guarded by a giant serpent, it would sound quite a bit like a pulp adventure plot. This fantastic legend sprang from the remains of Pecos Pueblo in northeastern New Mexico. While I had heard of the conquistadors' search for the Seven Cities of Gold in school, I didn't learn of Pecos Pueblo's fantastic past until adulthood. My childhood-self had definitely missed out. And Pecos Pueblo wasn't even the only one. There were many other "lost worlds," like Katzimo Mesa, that were completely unknown to me. Likewise, while I had been to White Sands, I had never heard the tale of the mythical pueblo that it concealed or of an Aztec outpost in El Capitan, a mountain I could see in the distance from my home.

In short, I never imagined so many strange places existed within the boundaries of New Mexico. The same might be true for you. If that's the case, then I hope you find this to be an enlightening read.

John LeMay

TABLE OF CONTENTS

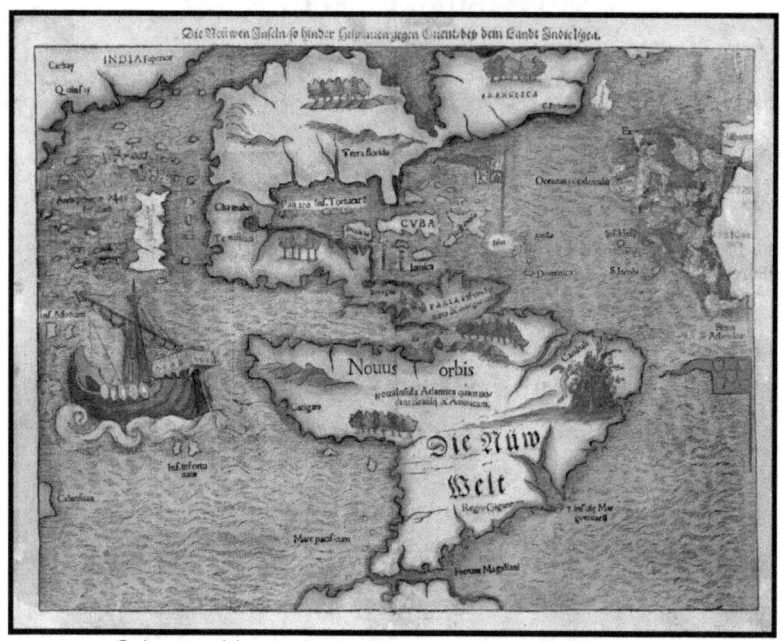

Sebastian Münster's 1540 map of the "New World."

INTRODUCTION
The New World

In the 16th century, the Americas were collectively known as *Mundus Novus*—the New World. To the Spanish conquistadors, it was *El Novo Mondo*. For them, it was the place where all their legends might come true. Among the strange and fantastic things thought to be found there were a race of giants, horn-blowing apes, and dog-snouted men who drank human blood.

The Spaniards were willing to risk these horrors for gold, for God, and for glory. That's because, somewhere in the New World, it was thought they might find St. Ursula and her 11,000 virgins on an island off the coast. In South America, they hoped to find El Dorado, the home of a king who rubbed his body in gold dust before submerging in a lake. And most importantly, they would seek the lost Seven Cities of Gold in the deserts of North America.

Juan Ponce de León was among the first and the most famous of the conquistadors, exploring what is today Florida in search of the Fountain of Youth in 1513. Today, some think Ponce de León believed in no such thing. While that's debatable, the Spanish conquistadors under the command of Hernán Cortés, conqueror of Mexico, absolutely believed that a land of riches awaited to the north. Somewhere in the deserts of what is today New Mexico, they were certain would be found the Seven Cities of Gold, also known as the Kingdom of Cibola.

As far as the Spaniards were concerned, the gold of the Aztecs would pale in comparison to the treasures awaiting discovery in the lands to the north. Cortés wanted to search them out himself but was bypassed in favor of an expedition led by Francisco Vázquez de Coronado.

This fanciful illustration shows pueblo ruins atop a mesa. Were they meant to represent Acoma, or something entirely fictitious?

This passage from *History of Arizona and New Mexico, 1530-1888*, by Hubert Howe Bancroft, summed up the myth of the Seven Cities of Gold quite well:

> ...the actual discoveries of 1539-43, as the years passed on, became semi-mythical, and were located anywhere to suit the writer's views, Indian villages being magnified without scruple into great cities; each new discovery on the frontier was described to meet requirements, and located where it would do the most good; and even the aborigines, as soon as they learned what kind of traditions pleased the white men most, did excellent service for the cause. Only a small portion of the current speculations and falsehoods found their

way into print, or have been preserved for our reading; but quite enough to show the spirit of the time.[1]

Though the Spaniards marveled at the remains of Chaco Canyon and the still populated but no less enigmatic Acoma Mesa, as we all know, they never found their Seven Cities of Gold. As such, the Kingdom of New Spain lost some of its mystique for a time. However, New Mexico regained some of its old mystery in the aftermath of the Mexican-American War of 1846-1848. To the Anglo newcomers, the ruins of the Spanish missions were just as awe-inspiring as the Anasazi cliff-dwellings were to the Spanish Conquistadors before them.

Above, in the distance, is pictured Mount Taylor, part of the San Mateo Mountain range. Located nearby was an old village hidden amidst the sands. In an article in the *San Francisco Chronicle*, early day explorer Charles Lummis noted how wind erosion had all but hidden the remains of the ruins near San Mateo: "One had also but to remember the ruin of San Mateo, so absolutely buried by the sands that the people who lived within gunshot of it never dreamed of its existence till a fierce sandstorm stripped some of the beautiful stone walls of it—to be dubious of a verdict rendered without digging."

In the absence of history, fantastic myths took hold. Good examples included the ruins of Gran Quivira, which early-day explorers thought had either been vacated due to the Pueblo

Revolt or a volcanic eruption, as evidenced by nearby lava flows. At the time, New Mexicans didn't know that the lava flow long predated the settlement, which was abandoned before the Pueblo Revolt of 1680 due to a myriad of unfortunate circumstances. Only upon the emergence of modern science and careful anthropological study did a clearer picture of the past begin to be painted and Gran Quivira's less adventurous history was revealed.

However, that didn't mean that fantastic legends had no basis in truth. As an example of the complete opposite, scholars of the late 19th century scoffed at tales of the people of Acoma Mesa having once inhabited the even taller Katzimo Mesa nearby. The Acomans claimed to have once lived atop the mesa until an intense storm destroyed the slope that allowed them to access it. Over the course of several explorations, it turned out that the mesa had been inhabited in some capacity in the past.

Within this book you will find similar tales of legends proven true along with cases of just the opposite, wherein misidentified ruins were bequeathed with fantastic mythologies that had no basis in fact. Whether the stories attached to them are true or not, in the pages ahead, prepare to explore New Mexico's many lost worlds and enchanted lands.

Section Notes

---

[1] Bancroft, *History of Arizona and New Mexico, 1530-1888*, pp.14-15.

ENCHANTED MESA
Pueblo Ruins of Katzimo

Sitting loftily atop Acoma Mesa 365 feet off the ground is Sky City. At over 2,000 years old, the pueblo is one of the oldest continually inhabited settlements in North America. But before that, the people of Acoma lived even higher off the ground on a similar settlement that they called Katzimo. Today, due to the legend and lore surrounding it, it is known as Enchanted Mesa.

Simply put, Enchanted Mesa lives up to its name. One of the earliest New Mexicans to write of its mystique was Charles Lummis, who described it as a "sandstone island left by the erosion which gouged out the valley" in what was then Valencia County. A 430-foot-high sandstone butte, some also appropriately called it the Gibraltar of the Southwest. Long and narrow in shape, Katzimo stretches 1,250 feet and is only 400 feet across at its widest point. It is called Katzimo or Kadzima by Acomans and other speakers of the Keresan language, while the Spaniards called it Mesa Encantada. The Acomans claimed that it was their original home until a great storm destroyed their only approach. That is why today the cliff is unscalable unless one is an experienced climber.

A short piece published in several newspapers in 1897 reported the egregious rumor that it "was popularly believed among Indians that a remnant of the ancient Aztec race were living up there still growing vegetables and keeping sheep."[1] As for other fantastic flourishes, apparently it was thought that perhaps the mesa might house some unique plant life as the article mentioned "the theory that the Enchanted Mesa is the only spot on earth where the flowers of long ago can exist without the contamination and the war of plant life of the present day."[2] There was also a hope of treasure atop the mesa in the form of gold and silver jewelry left behind by the previous residents of Katzimo.

Photo of Enchanted Mesa taken from Acoma Pueblo by W.H. Jackson in 1899.

While nothing as fantastic as that was believed by the Acomans themselves, they did claim that their ancestors hailed from Katzimo. According to Lummis in a *San Francisco Chronicle* article, "The top was reached, they say, by a great penol—a huge sliver split from the cliff and fallen against it."[3] He continued that it was extremely steep, and they cut toe holes in it to ascend. Lummis also said that the Acomans pointed out to him the spot where the "ladder rock" used to stand.

Water and crops grown in the valleys below had to be arduously hauled up the mesa. Some also theorized that wells or mini-reservoirs were created on the crest, so that enough water could be stored under the threat of a siege. But, what exactly happened to end the peaceful existence of the Acomans atop Enchanted Mesa?

According to their oral history, one fateful day all of the pueblo save for three women and a boy had ventured into the

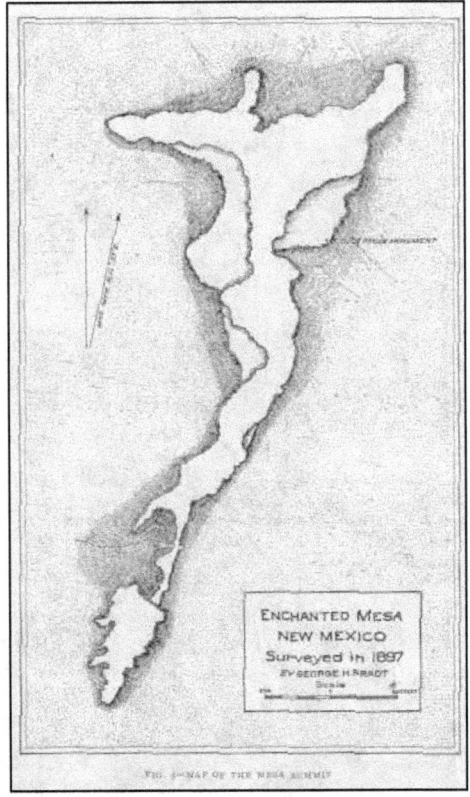

ENCHANTED MESA
NEW MEXICO
Surveyed in 1897
BY GEORGE H BRADT
Scale

FIG. 1—MAP OF THE MESA SUMMIT

valley below to work the fields.[4] The three women had been too ill to go to work that day, and so a youth named A-chi-te stayed behind to look after them. It was the summer monsoon season, and a catastrophic cloudburst struck the mesa so hard that it made some of the adobe dwellings crumble. In the chaos, A-chi-te pulled his mother from the rubble of their home and then decided to brave the hurricane force winds down the mesa to get help. As he did, the crushing torrent caused the great rock ladder to fall and shatter into pieces. As it was, the stone ladder's "base stood on a great hill of sand,"[5] hence how the intense rainfall eroded it away so swiftly.

Charles Lummis, one of the original sources closest to the period, received the tale of Enchanted Mesa from 98-year-old Acoma elder Martín Valle in 1892.

Charles Lummis, pictured above, was falsely accredited with scaling the mesa himself by several sources.

Lummis recounted the most fantastic part—which made the lost world lost—thusly,

> Suddenly he [A-chi-te] felt the ground quiver beneath his feet. A strange, rushing sound filled his ears; and, whirling about, he saw the great Ladder Rock rear, throw its head out from the cliff, reel there an instant in

mid-air, and then go toppling out into the plain like some wounded Titan. As those thousands of tons of rock smote upon the solid earth with a hideous roar, a great cloud went up, and the valley seemed to rock to and fro. From the face of the cliffs, three miles away, great rocks came leaping and thundering down, and the tall *piñons* swayed and bowed as before a hurricane... The Ladder Rock had fallen — the unprecedented flood had undermined its sandy bed![6]

According to folklore, after its desertion, the Enchanted Mesa became home to the evil Witch Society, which congregated in a cave on the north side of Enchanted Mesa.

The poor Acomans later tried in vain to scale the cliff not just to return to their old home but to rejoin the three women now stranded atop the great rock. Lummis told the papers, "The three women imprisoned above were seen for a long time. One, crazed by grief, flung herself off the cliff; the others finally starved."[7]

Some say sacrifices were made to a deity of some sort in hopes of returning to the top of the mesa, but they were all in vain.[8] "The spirits of those who died are still hovering over the 'Mesa Encantada' where they are destined to remain until Montezuma comes again to earth," one article dramatically concluded.[9]

THE ENCHANTED MESA.

Cincinnati Commercial Gazette (November 27, 1894).

Eventually, the former populace of Katzimo had no choice but to build a new home on a shorter mesa three miles away, which is today Acoma. It was Lummis who put forth the theory that if the walls could be scaled, evidence could be found of this ancient proto-Acoma atop Katzimo Mesa. Professor William Libbey of Princeton University heard Lummis's tale and set out to disprove it.

Much like a scene out of Sir Arthur Conan Doyle's *The Lost World*, the snarky professor announced to the press in 1897 that he would travel to faraway New Mexico to disprove the "Indian fairy story." An article from the same time fantastically claimed that a group of white men once tried to scale the mesa, but the Acomans ran them off before they could. Whether this is true or not is debatable, as that article seems to be the lone source of that story.[10] The same article wondered if Professor Libbey might encounter "superstitious opposition" himself upon arrival.

Later that year, and with no "superstitious opposition," Libbey ascended the mesa with a half dozen reporters in tow. Great lengths of rope, along with a pulley and a special chair, were used to hoist Libbey to the top, and a small cannon was used to shoot a coil of rope over the prow of the mesa. The ropes were then collected on the other side and tied to a team of horses. Up the professor went with a camera in tow, but it seems doubtful he intended to use it. One lucky newspaper man, identified only as Mr. Pearce, was sent up after him. Together, the duo explored the mesa for several hours.

At the top of Katzimo, though evidence was scattered all around Libbey, his skeptical agenda either hid the items from his eyes or he outright ignored them. What Libbey and his companion really found is unknown, but later it would be proven that remnants of a lost society was scattered across the mesa. However, when he returned from his journey, Libbey made the statement that "Romantic Indian legend can never stand the acid test of scientific investigation." Another article from the same time smugly concluded a write-up on the mesa, stating, "And now the Enchanted Mesa becomes the disenchanted mesa."[11]

In San Francisco, Lummis was asked about the discouraging news by the *Chronicle*. Lummis admitted, "I have had several hundred letters making suggestions or asking information about the Enchanted Mesa, but Professor Libbey's expedition is the first practical outcome of it all."[12] Lummis didn't entirely buy Libbey's verdict, though, and continued, "I have seen intelligent and observant men wholly unable to discover that they stood in what had been a stone pueblo and there are many sites which very few whites could make out without excavation." Lummis continued on to say that if an adobe pueblo as was supposed to exist at the top of the mesa had been "deverted" [sic] 600 years ago as the story alleged, then only the few specialists "who have given years of field study to these things could possibly decipher what would remain."[13]

Pottery shards and arrowheads later discovered atop Katzimo Mesa.

He also added, "I do not know how much training Professor Libbey has had in this line. It appears from the dispatches that he stayed but a short time on the summit, because a storm was coming up; and that he made no excavations whatever." Lummis also chided Libbey for not bothering to take an actual Acoman with him to the top of the mesa, as they would obviously know what to look for.

Interestingly, Lummis also noted three other mesas in the immediate region "upon which (so their legends relate) they had prehistoric pueblos—and the ruins are there to prove the story."[14]

Enchanted Mesa had a new layer added to its fantastic history when a UFO was seen over the mesa in the fall of 1974. The November 25, 1974 edition of the *Albuquerque Tribune* reported that a helicopter chartered by the crew of the "Nakia" TV series went to the top of the mesa to investigate. The sighting occurred on November 18th and was reported by Acoma police officer Bill Jopinkah. He said that he saw a "red light" sitting atop the mesa and that it "picked up like a helicopter, but much faster." Odder still, unlike a helicopter, it didn't make a sound. Another witness, this one from the Bureau of Indian Affairs and who wished to go unnamed, was quoted as seeing "a red light, 'faster than any aircraft I've ever seen'" as well. According to the article, several other Acoma patrolmen saw the "same thing on successive nights" that same week. Most accounts of the UFO tale like to end it right there and let the mystery linger. However, atop the mesa were later found the footprints of a large man who had appeared to be running when he made them. Landing marks of what looked to be another helicopter were also found, but it was felt that the landing marks were older than those of the man's footprints. As it was, the Bureau of Indian Affairs thought that perhaps the mesa was really just the drop-off zone for drug runners. But with all the lonely stretches of desert available across the Land of Enchantment, why pick the top of an unscalable mesa for the drop-off? Or, maybe that was the point. The drugs would be safely hidden there. All that said, it still doesn't explain why the patrolmen thought the fast-moving lights were a UFO and not a helicopter. And, are we to believe that over three different patrolmen really couldn't tell a helicopter from a UFO?

Frederick Webb Hodge, an archaeologist for the Smithsonian, read Libbey's account in the papers and smelt a rat, so he mounted his own expedition to the mesa.[15] As luck would have it, Hodge had already been directed by the Bureau of Ethnology to observe the Snake Dance of the Moki Indians. After this, he would be allowed to go to Enchanted Mesa, which he scaled on September 3, 1897. To aid him, Hodge recruited Major George H. Pradt, the deputy surveyor at Laguna Pueblo, plus a photographer, A.C. Vroman, and another man identified as H.C. Hoyt of Chicago. The wisest decision Hodge made over Libbey was in taking along two local men from the Laguna Pueblo, who unfortunately went unnamed in publications of the time.

Hodge's methods of scaling the mesa differed from Libbey's as well in that Hodge "procured an extension ladder, comprising six sections of six feet each together, with an ample supply of rope."[16] The papers reported that,

> The climb was without any serious difficulty until the party reached a great sandstone. The ladders were hauled section by section to this point by means of the ropes, then fitted together, and raised against the cliff. Mr. Hodge ascended to the top and climbing over the slope immediately above, lashed the top of the ladder to a huge bowlder [sic] that had fallen from above and lodged on the terrace some 20 feet from the summit. The ladder was then ascended by the remainder of the party and the top easily reached. The ascent consumed exactly 2¼ hours.[17]

The fact that Libbey never wanted to find anything atop the mesa was painfully evident when it was reported that Hodge found pottery shards within five minutes. Hodge and his crew then spent that afternoon and portions of the next day exploring Enchanted Mesa, discovering more pottery shards plus two stone axes, arrowheads, and other signs of habitation. The paper also supported claims of the storm that isolated the mesa, stating that the artifacts were found along the "narrow storm-swept crest." It continued, "All vestiges of the ancient trail ascending the talus and continued thence to the summit by hand and foot holes in the solid rock, have been obliterated, but some traces of the hole remain."[18]

In a calculated rebuff of Libbey's statement, Hodge said, "The Indian lore of a thousand years cannot be undone by a few hours of careless investigation." Lummis also heard of Hodge's triumph and noted that "Libbey's nonsense had been exposed, and Katzimo truly deserved its modern name – The Enchanted Mesa!"

MYSTERIOUS "ENCHANTED MESA" SCALED BY GIRLS

The mesa was climbed for the third time in 1921. Although it was the third climbing, it was a first in two other instances. It was the first time the mesa was scaled by nothing but rope, and the first time it was scaled by women. The climbers were Misses Erna Fergusson and Misses Hickey.

Chapter Notes

[1] *Eau Claire Leader* (September 7, 1897), p.3.

[2] *Montana Helena Independent* (August 13, 1897), p.2.

[3] Though it came from the *San Francisco Chronicle* originally, I retrieved it from the *Montana Helena Independent* of August 13, 1897.

[4] A variation of the story went that rather than only three women, three hundred people total perished atop the mesa that day, though the former is the more common version.

[5] Lummis, *A New Mexico David*, p.51.

[6] Ibid.

[7] *Montana Helena Independent* (August 13, 1897), p.2.

[8] It should be noted that the Navajo have a similar legend of their people once inhabiting Shiprock until one day a lightning strike broke away the trail leading to the top. Left behind were a number of women, children, and elderly who starved to death. As such, the Navajo discouraged the climbing of Shiprock lest anyone disturb the *chindi*, or ghosts, there.

[9] *Montana Helena Independent* (August 13, 1897), p.2. The reference to Montezuma related to a common Pueblo legend wherein the Aztec ruler Montezuma became conflated with a pueblo deity named Poseyemu who would supposedly return one day to free New Mexico from Spanish rule.

[10] *Salt Lake City Herald* (July 21, 1897), p.23.

[11] *Eau Claire Leader* (September 7, 1897), p.3.

[12] The *San Francisco Chronicle* via the *Montana Helena Independent* of August 13, 1897

[13] Ibid.

[14] Ibid.

[15] Though most accounts went that Libbey ascended the mesa first, followed by Hodge, I found an article that offered an alteration to this history printed in the *Gallup Independent* of August 12, 1947. It claimed that Hodge climbed to within 60 feet of the top of the mesa in 1895 and found a few pieces of pottery. This was then followed by Libbey's 1897 excursion, and then Hodge again that same year returned, went all the way to the top, and finally found evidence of habitation. Likewise, Howard Bryan said in his "Off the Beaten Path" column of April 9, 1962, that Charles Lummis was the first white man to scale the mesa and did so in 1883 via the use of toe and finger holes.

[16] *The Dalles Daily Chronicle* (February 11, 1899).

[17] Ibid.

[18] Ibid.

2

EL CAPITAN CAVE CITY
Lost World of Lincoln County

L incoln County will forever be remembered for the bloody range war of 1878, naturally known as the Lincoln County War. It made Billy the Kid a star and thanks to him and the war, the little village of Lincoln is now a state monument. Not only that, but all of Lincoln County capitalizes on the Kid and the war in some way or another. But even Lincoln County has its own lost world waiting to be found somewhere in the Capitan Mountains—and it has nothing to do with Billy the Kid.

According to area lore, an elaborate Aztec treasure city may lie hidden in the forests of Lincoln County. The fantastic story originated in the 16th century, during the Spanish conquest of the Aztec Empire in Mexico when Hernán Cortés took Emperor Montezuma prisoner in his own kingdom. At this time, Montezuma instructed a cavalcade of Aztecs to head north towards their mythical homeland of Aztlán and hide most of their gold. This way the evil invaders could never possess it. Various iterations of this tale concluded at different destinations, but one of the better-known ones was El Capitan Mountain near Ruidoso.

Years ago, I asked veteran treasure hunter Jack Purcell about the alleged Aztec treasure train. To my relief, he had heard of it before, and this was the reply:

When Cortés held Montezuma captive, the Aztec gave instructions that all Aztec gold be hidden from the Spaniards, so the legend goes and appears to be confirmed by the fact there was nowhere near the gold after the conquest there should have been. The legends say four groups of 1000 Aztecs each carried the treasures to different places in the north and hid them there.[1]

Postcard depicting the Capitan Mountains.

A similar account was given in an article appearing in the *Gold!* almanac of 1969 by Carl Howe entitled "Did the Dutchman find Montezuma's Treasure?" The author wrote of a researcher named Billy Glynn, who in 1892 went to Mexico to look through old military records. He discovered that Montezuma's successor, Guatomozin, sent a procession of riches northward to escape the Spaniards. According to Howe's article:

> This fabulous treasure was entrusted to the High Priest, who supervised its transfer to secret hiding places in the mountains. According to the legend, the treasure bearing slaves traveled in a northwesterly direction for many moons and then came to a mountain on the edge of a desert. There, in that gloomy, desolate place, the treasure was hidden and the slaves put to death and buried with the treasure. A curse was put upon the treasure and the mountain itself—a curse to be promptly invoked were the treasure ever to be molested.[2]

Though Howe was referring to Arizona in the previous quotation, his story lined up incredibly well with the treasure rumored to have been hidden by the Aztecs in the Capitan Mountains of New Mexico.[3]

It was said that the Aztecs knew of a cave that had been hollowed out by a long-dead race of giants to the north in what is today El Capitan

Aztec mummy.

Mountain, and so off they went.[4] Once the majestic Capitans were in sight of the nobles in charge of the Aztec caravan, they threatened the nearly one thousand slaves in their decree with death if the mountains were not reached by sundown. By the end of the day they reached the mountains, but in the process, many slaves perished from exhaustion and others from rattlesnake bites. On the morning of the next day, the Aztecs found the entrance to the lost cave of giants and made their way inside where they hid the treasure.

Most of the above tale was initially revealed by treasure hunter Wally Hesse, who related it in an old issue of *Treasure Search*. In his article, Hesse described the fantastic scene of the Aztecs hiding the gold thusly,

> For seventeen suns they labored, building a small city in this giant cavern. On the eighteenth day, the highest born king flung himself from the high cliff, to meet the gods and declare their wishes had been carried out. That night in the light of the full moon, the queen prepared herself and her two children to offer their hearts to their terrible gods. The stone altar inside the entrance changed slowly from a dull granite grey to a crimson red as the high priest held a large pulsating heart aloft and laid it gently beside the two smaller hearts which were now devoid of all movement.[5]

From then on, the queen and her children's mummified remains have allegedly watched over the entrance to the underground city built by the Aztec slaves. Upon leaving, the priest and the remaining slaves sealed the doorways so that no one else could enter or find the city. The caravan returned to Mexico with the idea that one day, when the Spanish invaders were driven away, they would return and reclaim their treasure.

Hesse became aware of this story when he placed an ad in the *Denver Post* stating that he had $1,000 to invest in a "valid mining venture." The most interesting answer Hesse received came from an old man in Roswell, who claimed to have found a lost Aztec treasure cave in the Capitan Mountains. The old man told Hesse how he had found a cave in the mountains with a flight of stone steps leading down them. However, he could only look into the cave, not descend into it as the opening was too small. The old man was reluctant to dynamite the entrance, which is why he responded to Hesse's ad in the *Denver Post*.

Hesse went down to Roswell with a jeep and some dynamite and the two traveled westward towards the Capitans. The old man's age, however, prevented him from being able to show Hesse the exact spot, as the land was too hard to traverse for the old timer, who had been younger when he first found the cave. "It's right over that ridge, Wally," the old man said to Hesse. "I can't make it. Go locate it. I'll take it slow and head back to camp."[6]

In the vast Capitans, Hesse was unable to find the cave the old man claimed was just over the ridge and decided to go back to camp. The next morning, they heard over the radio that a heavy snow was coming and decided to go back home and try again later.

In the years to follow, Hesse kept in touch with the old man and before he died, he told Hesse in greater detail what the formations near the cave opening looked like. Hesse kept researching the old man's claims even after he had died and said that he found many facts corroborating the old man's story, although he never stated in his article just what those facts were.

On a return trip to the area, Hesse said that he found an old poplar tree with carved markings of an Indian in full headgear, a turtle, and an arrow carved into it. It is common knowledge to treasure hunters that turtles often represent treasure. And, the arrow carved into the tree pointed in the same direction the old man claimed the cave was located. Hesse cut the portion out of the tree and with help from a friend in Ruidoso took it to Eugene Chihuahua, a well-known Apache living at the Mescalero Apache Indian Reservation.[7] Chihuahua was born in the early 1880s, and had lived an adventurous life during the time of Geronimo. Chihuahua was a very knowledgeable man and an integral source of information for historian Eve Ball on the history and ways of the Apache. In other words, he was a very reliable source. Upon inspecting the sample brought to him by Hesse, Chihuahua said that the signs either pointed to treasure, water, or possibly both.

Later, Hesse said he found a giant rock formation that bared similarities to a turtle in alignment with the arrow's point. Eventually, Hesse mounted a formal expedition to find the cave entrance with a European mountain climber, Kurt Richardson, and an English illustrator, Julia Purcell, to map out the rock formations. The trio got close to finding the area on the very last night of the expedition, but with supplies running low, they had to turn back the next morning. Hesse's article ended optimistically stating that one day he planned to return to the site and find the hidden city of the Aztecs once and for all.

Apparently, Hesse never found the treasure, and so far he is the only one to have ever written about it extensively. "It's kind of hard to believe that a legend with hundreds of years of folk-to-folk mileage would not at the very least hold some truth," said Mickey Cochran, a long-time Ruidoso resident. When I asked him about the treasure, he told me,

I believe even the Lost Dutchman's Mine pales in comparison to the Capitan Treasure Cave both in value and validity. Yet, the Capitan Treasure Cave isn't near as famous ... and, surprisingly, it's quite difficult to find

31

any historical documentation. It's almost as if this treasure's history has been long hidden from the public... which makes it even more mysterious and intriguing.[8]

Photo by Skyler Link of pictographs in the Capitans, this one indicating two chambers of gold and a mining shaft.

Cochran also met someone who had a similar story to Hesse's:

I have personally met someone, back when I worked as an in-house artist for Bounty Hunter Metal Detectors, who claimed with full astuteness, that he had spent half his lifetime looking for this particular cave ... and in the process, had discovered symbols carved in rock that denoted this particular Aztec treasure was in close proximity to where he was hunting. He was in search of a gravitometer at the time ... for he believed that the cave was well buried or maybe even caved in by the Aztecs. Thusly, the only way he would discover this treasure would be via a way to measure gravitational pull with the hopes of revealing cavities in the earth.

Lost Mine Found.

The Roswell papers tell of the discovery of a lost mine in the east end of the Capitan mountains, this county. The finders are Dr. T. E. Pressley and J. A. Norman, of Roswell, the latter a one-time resident of this county. The value of the find has not yet been ascertained, but a partly-filled-in shaft, unknown to the residents of the locality, was uncovered, which led to the belief that it had been worked as a mine perhaps a hundred years ago. We hope it will prove valuable, put generally lost mines remain lost.

The above clipping, from the *Carrizozo News* of March 10, 1911, might allude to the lost treasure cave of the Capitans.

Several Roswell residents have also heard similar stories about a cave in the mountains with a series of stone steps descending to an underground city. Jack Purcell also heard of the lost treasure of the Capitans but remained more skeptical when asked for his opinion on it. "I suspect the Capitans story ain't a good one, though I suppose it might be. Maybe the Aztecs had an outpost up there somewhere and were mining on that side of the Rio Grande, also," Purcell mused.

Since writing about this story several years ago, my friend, Skyler Link, who is very familiar with the Capitan region, told me of rock glyphs he has seen and photographed himself that would seem to be the same ones that Hesse found. Link knows of a man who claimed to find an Aztec or Incan-like statue of a turtle-like man raising his hands in the air. It was found in the region of Saw Mill Canyon in the Capitans. Since turtles indicate treasure, and a hands-up stance can signify war, perhaps this statue was created during the Spanish invasion of the Aztec Empire. Thus, it nicely conjoins the story of the Aztec procession carrying treasure away from the conflict to the Capitans.

Photo by Skyler Link of gold sign and anchor.

Actually, the treasure-glyphs spread throughout the Capitans found by Link appear to be related more to the Spanish than the Aztecs. One photo, taken by Link, depicts a circle sign surrounded by dots, which can indicate *varas*—Spanish units of measurement. Another depicts a Spanish sign for gold with an anchor next to it, which signifies something below.[9] Because of this, an alteration to the Aztec tale emerged wherein the Aztec party was killed, and it was the Spanish who hid the Aztec gold, not the Aztecs.

Whether Aztec or Spanish, is a secret underground treasure city waiting to be found in the Capitans? Only the mountains know for certain, and they aren't telling.

Chapter Notes

[1] Email to the author.

[2] Howe, *Gold!*, p.41..

[3] Though Glynn mentioned only one group, Purcell mentioned four columns consisting of one thousand Aztecs that set out in different directions. One of these caravans has been proposed as the source of the mysterious gold rumored to reside in Victorio Peak, currently nestled in the confines of White Sands Missile Range.

[4] According to Aztec myth, seven giants survived their version of the Great Flood by carving tunnels into the earth. They were led by one named Xelhua, who later carved the tunnels beneath the Great Pyramid of Cholula in Mexico according to legend.

[5] Hesse, "Capitan's Gold," *Treasure Search*, n.d.

[6] Ibid.

[7] Considering Chihuahua passed away in 1965, that would imply that Hesse's adventure took place in either the 1960s or possibly the 1950s.

[8] Email to the author.

[9] In addition to Capitan, there also appear to be some treasure markings relating to Fort Stanton Cave.

Spiral petroglyph at Three Rivers. (author's photo)

3

THREE RIVERS PETROGLYPHS
Story on the Rocks

ocated seventeen miles north of Tularosa is Three
Rivers Petroglyph Site.[1] Comprised of Paleozoic rock
stretching between the San Andres and Sacramento
Mountains, 21,000 examples of Jornada Mogollon art are
etched onto the rocks. The petroglyphs are believed to have
been created between 200-1450 A.D. by stone tools that
removed the dark patina, sometimes called "desert varnish,"
from the exterior of the rocks to create the white carvings.

The carvings feature representations of many familiar
symbols. There are spiral designs common to many Native
American petroglyph sites, numerous handprints, a handful
of thunderbirds, masks, sunbursts, and a few mountain goats
that look suspiciously like dinosaurs to some. More than
anything, the sheer number of petroglyphs concentrated at
one site made it one of the most significant archeological
finds of the entire Southwest.

Though not quite as mysterious as the disappearance of the
Anasazi, Three Rivers once hosted an enigmatic population
of its own, and it appears that the area has been occupied and
abandoned several times by different tribes. For instance, an
archeological excavation conducted in April of 1925 by the El
Paso Archeological Society found that some of the pueblo
remains appeared to have been burned and the last signs of
habitation appeared to date to 1350.

Some of the rock art at Three Rivers. (author's photo)

All that experts can agree on is that the area was inhabited by the Jornada Mogollon people. Who they really were, much like the Anasazi, is a bit of a mystery. Most archaeologists consider the Jornada Mogollon to be the predecessors of the Puebloans, who presumably descended from them. However, there used to be a widely held belief among archeologists and anthropologists of the 19th century that the Puebloans were related to the Aztecs. This was also due to the fact that the Aztecs themselves said that they hailed from a land to the north. Specifically, like many Native American tribes, they claimed to have emerged from a cave, in their case called Aztlán, to come to the surface world. From that still-unknown spot somewhere in North America, they journeyed southward to Mexico.

Just as an example, and there are many others, the *Kansas City Journal* of October 27, 1880, stated that

> There seems to be no doubt that the Aztecs migrated from some more northern region into Mexico, and the traditions of the present Pueblos, who are believed to be descendants of the original Aztecs, teach that this very spot [New Mexico] was the birth place of Montezuma.

Three Rivers and the surrounding landscape. (author's photo)

The Inter Ocean of August 22, 1897, out of Chicago, likewise reported

> It is also still the custom of most writers to refer to the ruins and relics of [New Mexico and Arizona] as undoubtedly of Aztec origin, and to adopt more or less fully the theory that the ancestors of the Pueblo tribes were Aztecs left in Arizona during the famous migration from the north-west to Mexico.

Though the Aztec theory was brushed off and forgotten over time, Three Rivers might actually present the best evidence of all for connections to the Aztec. That's because, interestingly, at Three Rivers, several depictions of the Aztec deity of Tláloc, a rain god, can be found.[2]

Archaeologist Polly Schaafsma, one of the leading experts on prehistoric rock art, believes that the Three Rivers petroglyphs are linked to the nearby pueblo remains in a socio-religious sense, though. Others think that the petroglyphs tell a religious story if read in the right order and bears the most resemblance to the story of the Hopi, who primarily reside in northeastern Arizona.

The main proponent of this theory is Tularosa area archaeologist Joe Ben Sanders, who has spent much of his life studying the petroglyphs. Sanders' intriguing theory is that the Jornada Mogollon people migrated to Three Rivers from Casas Grandes in northern Mexico. His theory is that Casa Grandes was the place that the Hopi called Palatkwapi. Translating to the "Red House," Palatkwapi was the Hopi's peaceful city of origin, which they were forced to flee. Sanders believes that certain rock carvings resemble the various clans of the Hopi plus the distinctive kachina people of their oral histories.

Depiction of a ram, which looks like a duckbilled dinosaur to some.

Also among the rock carvings are what appear to be the Hopi Hero Twins, Tawahongva and Tawiayisnima. However, the Hero Twins are a common fixture of many Native American tribes in North America and also those of Mesoamerica—including the Aztecs. Therein lies part of the problem. As it stands, the religious stories of the Hopi, the Aztecs, and other tribes of North America and Mesoamerica always had similar ideas. For instance, all believe that there have been four to five major world cataclysms, the last of which was the great flood. Many have mystical water serpents that bring the rain, the monster-slaying Hero Twins, and so on. For all we know, the Three Rivers Petroglyphs might well be telling their own unique variation of these common myths. As Gary Cozzens put it in *Tres Ritos: A History of Three Rivers, New Mexico*, "Interpretation of the rock art is controversial at best. Best theories support the linkage of the Three Rivers site with worship of the Mexican deities Tlaloc and Quetzalcoatl."[3]

Could Three Rivers ironically be the missing proof long sought for a connection between the Aztecs and the Pueblos? Is Sanders correct that it is specifically related to the Hopi? Or does the mysterious rock art tell its own unique version of some lost tribe's origin? Until someone truly learns how to interpret the rocks, we may never know.

Chapter Notes

[1] Tres Ritos in the original Spanish, the area derives its name from the Indian Creek, Golodrina, and Three Rivers Creek rivers.

[2] In *Tres Ritos: A History of Three Rivers, New Mexico*, author Gary Cozzens noted on page 18 that, "Prominent among the designs of the Three Rivers Mogollon was Tlaloc, a goggle-eyed rain god of Mesoamerica."

[3] Cozzens, *Tres Ritos*, p.24.

FORT SUMNER'S PETRIFIED FOREST

According to the Navajo, the prehistoric trees at Arizona's Petrified Forest National Park are actually the bones of the giant Yé'iitsoh. When the Navajo were tragically forced to settle within Fort Sumner's Bosque Redondo in the 1860s, unbeknownst to them was another petrified forest to the north of them. Had they seen the petrified trees of Fort Sumner, it would have been interesting to see if they interpreted them the same way. *The Albuquerque Morning Journal* of June 18, 1911, reported how a register of the land office, A.E. Curren, had taken a fishing trip along the Pecos River twenty miles north of Fort Sumner when he discovered the petrified forest. The petrified remains were found on the left bank of the Pecos looking north, and the paper described them as petrified cedar trees that must have been "giants in their day" and some of the fallen trunks measured more than three feet in diameter:

> The specimens are in a remarkable state of preservation, some of them having their branches intact. Except for their weight and hardness, no one would suspect that they had not died during the last ten years. It has been suggested that the discovery be mentioned to the department of the interior, with a view to having the land upon which the trees are lying, which is considerable extent, set aside as a national monument, as has been done with the petrified forest in Arizona.

The next article to chronicle the petrified forest was published in *The Fort Sumner Review* on July 29, 1911. It read:

> A letter was received by us from the Bureau of Immigration asking whether there was a "petrified forest" near Ft. Sumner. The *Socorro Chieftain* also writes of the developments of this story, which was told by Register A. E. Curren, of the U.S. Land Office, upon the return from his fishing trip. Although the story was told after the trip up the Pecos river, it is not a "fish story"; as we have inquired and have found out of such a forest and have been informed in the affirmative.
>
> This forest lies about twenty miles north of Ft Sumner and it is there, and those who may have drifted from the "mule state" have only to put on their khaki suits and make a trip to Ft Sumner and from here three or four hours ride will show them that it is no after dinner fish story.
>
> The forest is not a large one but it is there.

Sadly, no national monument ever resulted from the remains, and today they are mostly forgotten.

4

THE HAUNTED MESA
Urraca Mesa's Gate to Hell

The concept of parallel dimensions has been a staple of science fiction for years. While you would expect such subject matter in sci-fi, you would not expect it from the quintessential Western novelist Louis L'Amour. And yet, in one of his final novels, *The Haunted Mesa*, he crafted a tale about a lost civilization existing in a parallel universe inhabited by the Anasazi. L'Amour became inspired to write the story, then called "No Man's Mesa," after allegedly climbing the real No Man's Mesa in Utah.

In the late 1920s, L'Amour had just been laid off from the Katherine Mine in Arizona. He and another miner from Kingman were traveling to Colorado along Route 66. In a diner in Flagstaff, L'Amour had a chance meeting with an old cowboy who ended up inspiring what became *The Haunted Mesa*. In conversation, L'Amour mentioned heading towards Navajo Mountain in Utah, which elicited a strong reaction from the man. He stated that he used to punch cows in that region but would never return. When pressed for details, all the man would say was that he "saw some things over there that nobody should see."[1] When L'Amour asked him again to be more specific, all the old cowboy would say was that it had something to do with No Man's Mesa.

L'Amour on the trail.

And so, L'Amour and his miner companion went to No Man's Mesa. One night, some of the miner's friends from the Paiute tribe came to visit. When L'Amour asked them about No Man's Mesa, they seemed curiously evasive on the subject. Finally, one of the younger men in the party let slip to L'Amour that there was a trail he could climb to the top, which he did soon after. According to conflicting accounts, L'Amour either found strange ruins atop the mesa, or nothing at all. In the special edition of *The Haunted Mesa*, L'Amour's journal revealed that while atop No Man's Mesa, L'Amour was haunted by a "very eerie unusual feeling"[2] and that he came down soon after, never forgetting the place.

Many years later, in the late 1970s and early 1980s, Beau L'Amour, Louis' son, recalled researching the gestating novel with his father. Together, they explored Anasazi ruins, and Beau remembered hearing many tales of "haunted buildings, Navajo witchcraft, and strange animals."[3]

Chaco Canyon in San Juan County, New Mexico.

L'Amour was further fascinated with the Anasazi after attending the Pecos Conference. There, he talked to several of the archeologists who had worked on Mesa Verde and Chaco Canyon. The idea that the sipapus represented gateways to the underworld intrigued him, and L'Amour pondered a concept wherein the Anasazi disappeared into another dimension.

Though L'Amour's fictional mesa in his novel was predominantly based upon No Man's Mesa in Utah, one could argue it was a pastiche of several such mesas. New Mexico's version of "the Haunted Mesa" would undoubtedly be Urraca Mesa outside of Cimarron. The mesa is two miles long and a half a mile wide and located along the southeastern corner of the huge Philmont Scout Ranch, a Boy Scouts of America-owned campground. It is a basalt-capped plateau, and a steep-sided one at that. Atop it is a sea of ponderosas, and amidst the trees are hidden ruins and petroglyphs. It is also the abode of black bears and mountain lions. Most of all, it is known for the magpie birds, or urracas, which give the mesa its name.

Vintage postcard depicting Philmont Scout Ranch,
photographed by Dan Sheehan in 1965.

The first clue that something ominous lies upon the mesa can be seen when one views it via a topographical map. If so, one will notice that the westernmost end of the mesa bulges out and becomes unusually unlevel for the mostly flat mesa. And it looks quite a bit like a human skull. It is in the eye of the giant skull that the portal to the netherworld is said to be located. Whether the portal leads to hell, as most would call it, or a previous world is debatable. Most Native American tribes believe in many past worlds that their tribes had to journey to. Along those lines, a local legend said the Anasazi disappeared into another world via a portal on Urraca Mesa.

For context, to this day, none of the experts can settle on a reason for the disappearance of the Anasazi, the ancient civilization that occupied Chaco Canyon and other settlements across the Southwest. Some think that they were driven away by the Toltecs, and others have postulated that an unknown illness wiped them out. Whatever the case, they certainly disappeared without a trace, which is where Urraca Mesa comes in.

As usual, there are many variations of the tale of Urraca Mesa, its occupation by the Anasazi, and its rediscovery by the Navajo. As such, something of a pastiche will be presented here. About two hundred years ago, a lone Navajo

46

medicine man found himself drawn to a flock of magpies. (The magpie was thought of as a trickster and a messenger to the Navajo.) It is said that the noisy birds congregated in the pinon trees near his hogan, demanding that he follow them. The magpies led the medicine man—or men, depending on the version—miles away for several days until they arrived at Urraca Mesa. Upon first seeing it, the medicine man was filled with a sense of unease as he could feel dark energy coming from the spot. Eventually, they led him to the great sandstone wall that told the tale of the Anasazi.

Spiral petroglyph on Urraca Mesa.

The full story went that an epic "final battle" took place there between the good people of earth and all the evil spirits from the underworld. A more specific version stated that the two factions had leaders in the form of the good Lord of the Outerworld and his evil twin brother, the Lord of the Underworld.[4] Though the Lord of the Outerworld banished his evil twin back to hell, the Anasazi unfortunately went with him into this alternate dimension, forever lost. Upon interpreting this story in the rocks, the medicine man decided that something had to be done to keep the portal to hell sealed so that it could never open again. To do so, he intricately carved four cat totems out of wood and placed them strategically at the four corners of the mesa.[5]

47

As an added security measure, the medicine man decided to stay there forever to protect the totems. Supposedly he can still be seen today as a blue-tinted ghost, a glowing orb, or in the forms of animals, typically a panther or bear. Today, only two of the four totems remain, leading some to think that if the other two fall or disappear that hell might overflow onto earth. And indeed, if reports are to be believed, some evil spirits and monsters make their way out of the portal occasionally.

Among the strange beings glimpsed atop the mesa is a three-foot-tall, pitch-black dwarf that sprints from tree to tree. Sometimes, it also appears in people's tents. Texas's Stampede Mesa is probably the spot most associated with "Ghost Riders in the Sky," but Urraca Mesa also sports a supernatural herd of horses stampeding through the skies. Yet another unverified source seemed to imply something akin to the Tombstone Thunderbird flying over the mesa.[6]

The most famous ghost to haunt the mesa is that of Black Jack Ketchum, an outlaw who held up several trains and notoriously had his head ripped off when his hanging was botched in Clayton, New Mexico, in 1901. Many years later, in the vicinity of the Philmont Scout Ranch, a boy scout troop was backpacking across the mountains to visit sites of historical interest, among them an abandoned gold mine and a ghost town. They also visited a large rock overhang hideout alleged to have been used by Black Jack Ketchum. The boys wanted to camp under the overhang, but the scoutmaster wouldn't let them and insisted they camp at a designated spot nearby. That night, five of the boys snuck away to the hideout to set up their own camp. Under the overhang, they built a fire and discussed their journey so far. Eventually, they all fell asleep. One of the boys, the unnamed storyteller of the tale, claimed that noises from the bushes nearby woke him up. Upon waking, he experienced the phenomenon known as sleep paralysis, where he was conscious but unable to move or speak.

Then he saw the source of the noise: a filthy, dirty cowboy dressed in all black. His face glistened red, as though scorched by the sun even in the darkness of night. The figure was mostly solid, though a few parts of his body appeared to be translucent. The boy took note of the man's clothes, which looked tattered and ancient as though they were from the days of the Wild West, and also of the fact that the man carried a revolver. Luckily for the boy, the phantom cowboy didn't seem to notice him. In fact, it was as if the boy was seeing into another dimension occupied by the cowboy.

Ketchum's 1901 hanging in Clayton, New Mexico.

The boy claimed that a mist began to emanate from a tree line across from a small stream. From within the mist, he could hear the shouts of men and also gunfire. The cowboy turned his attention to the noise and fired his revolver in the direction of the mist. The cowboy then ran right to where the boy slept and began firing while standing right above him. During the shooting, the man was hit by a bullet in the shoulder. As he returned fire, the terrified scout watched as the bullet casings fell to the ground next to where he lay.

Suddenly, for the first time, the gunslinger noticed the scout beneath his feet. The outlaw looked nearly as startled as the boy and muttered, "You're not supposed to be here." After that, the cowboy ghost disappeared into thin air. The next morning, the boy told his fellow scouts what had happened, though they simply brushed it off as him pulling a prank. Later in the trip, upon stopping in an Old West-themed saloon, the boy saw a picture on the wall of the cowboy from his experience. It was Black Jack Ketchum.

Speaking of time portals, coincidentally, early travelers along the Santa Fe Trail named one of the landmarks the Tooth of Time. Standing at 9,003 feet, the Tooth of Time is a dacite monolith, composed of two laccoliths, protruding 500 feet vertically into the air.

Rather than ghosts, some think these spectral figures are really glimpses into the past. Case in point, in 2003 an account appeared online telling of a former Philmont staff member who camped atop the mesa one night. He awoke during a rainstorm and sighted a blue vertical line that materialized a few feet off the ground and then dropped down like a curtain. Out of this apparent time portal came a group of Native Americans charging on horseback. The man fled in terror and accidentally ran into a barbed-wire fence and bled to death... which is, unfortunately, exactly why this is befitting of an online tale. Because, if the man died, how did anyone learn his story? Perhaps his ghost told it.

Some treasure hunters have speculated that Urraca Mesa may hold a secret gold cache due to the many lightning strikes it receives.

While that story is a bit discouraging, it seems to be based on more credible accounts of strange blue lights along the mesa. Others tell of missing time, similar to UFO abductions. Some campers reported feelings of time and distance being strangely distorted when they were there. For instance, perhaps a two-hour hike felt more like four, or the trail might seem to twist and distort in strange ways. Compasses also do not work on the mesa, and batteries drain quickly.

If the story of the scout who saw Black Jack is to be believed, then it would seem that the area is home to some sort of time portal. This is because, as the scout was putting up his bedroll the morning after the encounter, he found six shell casings in the dirt next to him. Were these perhaps shell casings from the Old West? The boy naturally swiped the shells to keep as a memento. When he had them examined by a gun expert, the gunsmith confirmed that they were indeed from 1878, but appeared to be brand new at the same time. Furthermore, the gunpowder used to fire the bullets was also of an old variety, but the casings appeared to have been fired very recently, as gunpowder could still be smelt on them. Whether or not any of this is true is naturally unverifiable, but that's the story in a nutshell.

The wild town of Cimarron is the nearest settlement in the vicinity of Urraca Mesa. Cimarron was the stomping grounds of gunfighters like Clay Allison and was also visited by the likes of Black Jack Ketchum, Kit Carson, Annie Oakley, Wyatt Earp, and Jesse James. Undoubtedly one of the wildest towns of the Wild West, the *Las Vegas Gazette* once quipped, "Everything is quiet at Cimarron. Nobody has been killed in three days." Cimarron's own pastor was even found shot dead in Cimarron Canyon during the Colfax County War, which raged from 1873 to 1888.

The most likely explanation for the mesa's paranormal attributes is the fact that its walls are laced with heavy amounts of magnetite and iron. As such, lightning strikes are more frequent on the mesa than they are at other places. Actually, lightning strikes there more than any other place in New Mexico. The high amount of magnetite might also be why so many hikers and campers report malfunctioning compasses. That said, in 1968, a geologist by the name of F. Leo Misaqi studied the mesa with an eye towards its stranger attributes. He could only conclude that "There is no simple explanation for [the] geochemical anomalies...."

Stranger yet, photos taken atop the mesa back in the days of film cameras tended to develop in a distorted way. Other times, cameras picked up a strange blue glow along the rim of the mesa. Perhaps it was merely the spectral shaman, said to have a ghostly blue energy about him, simply doing his job to guard the mesa...

Chapter Notes

---

[1] L'Amour, Louis L'Amour's Lost Treasures: *The Haunted Mesa* (Bonus Material), p.445.

[2] Ibid, p.446.

[3] Ibid, p.448.

[4] Hudnall, *Spirits of the Border*, p.186.

[5] Another variation says there were six total and were built by the Anasazi themselves. In this version, four still remained and the medicine man decided to stay there forever to protect the remaining totems.

[6] In 1890, the *Tombstone Epitaph* ran a now infamous story about two ranchers shooting a large, pterodactyl-like creature in the deserts of Arizona.

Ellis Wright, c.1932, who discovered a set of mysterious stone footprints along the White Sands. Initially, they were thought to have been the footsteps of a giant, but recent finds indicate that they were made by a prehistoric giant ground sloth. (Above courtesy Wright's niece, Terri Bunt, and also the image on page 56.)

5

LOST WORLD OF WHITE SANDS
Hidden City Beneath the Sands

According to legend, the land currently covered with the white sands was once a fertile oasis overseen by a small pueblo. As with most fairy-tale civilizations, this pueblo was peaceful and loving. They had no disputes with other tribes and they worshipped "the Sun Father, the Earth Mother and the many manifestations of nature as well as life in all its forms."[1] All was well until one night one of their medicine men had what was either a prophetic dream or an apocalyptic vision. In it, he saw a "great canoe" with "white wings that did not flap in the breeze,"[2] obviously a sailing ship. The occupants had long hair on their faces, hanging down to their chests. And they rode upon strange animals which, though four-footed and hooved like antelopes, were larger and fiercer. The men wore strange metal blankets over their chests that clanked as they walked.

The medicine man's vision was that of the Spanish conquistadors, who had landed on the shores of Mexico and would eventually make their way north to their pueblo. The shaman called a meeting at the plaza of the pueblo and told the people of his fearsome vision. As this was a peaceful pueblo, prayer rather than war was decided upon. A young hunter and a young maiden journeyed to a sacred altar located atop the nearby San Andres mountains.

The White Sands region was rife with prehistoric discoveries in the 1930s (one obscure article even mentioned finding dinosaur petroglyphs). In the U.S. Department of the Interior booklet, *The Story of the Great White Sands*, it was written:

> In the fall of 1932 Ellis Wright, a government trapper, reported that he had found human tracks of unbelievable size imprinted in the gypsum rock on the west side of White Sands. At his suggestion a party was made to investigate. Mr. Wright served as guide, O. Fred Arthur, Supervisor of the Lincoln National Forest, Edgar Cadwalader and one of his sons from Mountain Park, and the writer made up the party. As Mr. Wright had reported there were 13 tracks crossing a narrow swag, pretty well out between the mountains and the sands. Each track was approximately 22 inches long and from 8 to 10 inches wide. It was the consensus that the tracks were made by a human being, for the print was perfect and even the instep plainly marked. However there was not one in the group who cared to venture a guess as to when the tracks were made or how they became of their tremendous size. It is one of the unsolved mysteries of the Great White Sands.

In 1981, a group from the New Mexico Bureau of Mines and Mineral Resources studied the footprints and deduced the prints didn't belong to a giant human, but rather a prehistoric mammoth, a prehistoric camel, and another unidentified mammal made in the Pleistocene era. Even more recently, it has been determined that the tracks of the "giant" were actually those of a giant sloth being pursued by ice age hunters.

White Sands National Monument with the San Andres Mountains in the background. (Historical Society for Southeast New Mexico)

Down below, back in the pueblo, the people danced and prayed in the plaza as well. Atop the holy altar, the hunter and the maiden used the "most potent of their magic" in "making the prayer plumes they were to carry" along with sacred plumes of cedar.[3] The two young people sat with their legs crossed and their heads bowed before the altar. They, too, had the same vision as that of the medicine man of the Spaniards. Worse yet, they were told that there was no way to stop them. Not only would they subjugate the pueblo and change their way of life, but they even carried with them diseases that their pure immune systems could not withstand. In *Monumental Ghosts*, Alice Bullock related,

"What can we do?" asked the pair. "Is there no way for us?"

"You have been good people," the soft, sighing wind in the trees told them.

"Go back to the pueblo. Gather all the people and tell them that they are to sleep inside the pueblo tonight - not on the roof nor in the fields. Put the turkeys in their pens and cover the ceremonial eagles with mantas. Tie the dogs securely. Cover all the fires until not a spark is left. No one is to look out the doors or leave his sleeping blanket for any reason."

"We, your gods, cannot keep the strangers away. All we can do is save you until they are gone. That will be a long, long time, but you will sleep happily and it will seem but a night to you."[4]

Similar to tales of a lost civilization buried beneath White Sands are tales of ancient ruins beneath the Valley of Fires. *The Ruidoso News* of March 16, 1951, told tales of gold guarded by a nest of rattlesnakes in a volcanic crater and also spoke of a lost civilization smothered by the molten lava:

> The lava flow apparently covered the remains of an ancient Indian civilization for beneath the surface are found... and have been found ... many remains of Indian villages.

Not quite sure what that meant, the young people retuned to the pueblo. Although the people were hoping for a more affirmative answer, they had enough faith in their gods to do as told. That night, a new moon rose over the pueblo, and from the skies rained and drifted down a mist of glistening white crystal sand. Gently, one by one, the white crystal beads covered the pueblo and the surrounding land until it was completely buried under the white sands.

Not long after, as the Spaniards marched along the Jornada del Muerto, they saw no peaceful pueblo, only a strange sea of white sand, unlike anything they had seen before. Today, the peaceful pueblo sleeps beneath the sands, and when the invader is finally gone, its residents will awaken and resume their old lifestyle.

Another "Indian Legend" pertaining to the sands was printed in the *Alamogordo News* of January 13, 1927. It stated that:

> According to Indian legend this valley was once the bed of the "father of waters," along whose banks there dwelled in great numbers a prosperous race. Then came, according to the legend, "the year of fire during which the river ceased to flow. Poison gases and flames wasted the surrounding territory leaving death in its wake. Drout followed, which changed the once fertile valley into a barren desert and forced the survivors of the flames to seek refuge elsewhere.
>
> To substantiate the Indian legend, just above the sand, a vast lava flow of recent origin is to be found, while more recent and authentic tradition tells of rushing waters that were, and of ancient villages, now buried in the sands which have relentlessly swept over them, obliterating all traces of their existence.

In addition to the phantom pueblo, White Sands begat many other ghostly disappearances. The most famous of these was undoubtedly that of Albert J. Fountain and his eight-year-old son, Henry. Fountain was a prominent territorial lawyer who had just served indictments against several cattle rustlers in late January of 1896. Fountain had traveled from Mesilla to Lincoln to do so. He and Henry were last seen traveling across the White Sands. They were never seen again. Their wagon, however, was found stained with blood. The bodies are still missing to this day, though occasionally someone will claim to have found them.

2273 "Billy The Kid", New Mexico's Notorious Outlaw

One of the strangest legends pertaining to both the sands and the disappearance of Albert J. Fountain appeared in the book *The Young Pioneer When Captain Tom was a Boy*. Although passed off for a time as non-fiction, it was penny-dreadful fiction at its best. In the book, Billy the Kid warns Fountain not to venture into the White Sands—never mind that Billy had been dead fifteen years by then. When Fountain and his son are killed and buried in the sands by the Tate Gang, Billy witnesses the event. After this, Billy becomes "The Mounted Ghost of Crawling White Sands" who cannot leave the area until he avenges Fountain by killing all of the gang's members. Billy stays at a mythical Indian oasis on the sands and wears a white robe while riding a white horse to extract his vengeance. If the "mythical Indian oasis" was based on the hidden pueblo described earlier, or if it was a product of the author's imagination, is unknown.

And though many people have been murdered along White Sands, sometimes they seem to disappear into thin air. White Sands' most famous ghost is not unlike the river haunting woman in white called La Llorona. Only in the case of Pavla Blanca, the woman in white is associated with earth rather than water.[5] Bula Charles wrote of seeing the ghost with her husband, Tom, at White Sands in her booklet, *Tales of the Tularosa*.

> ...in the midst of the silence, the wind breathed. I could hear it sighing across the sand. I could feel it, half-hot, half-cool. A swirling eddy swept up a long slope off to the left, like a dust devil on a hot day. But it wasn't like a dust devil.
> "Look." Tom was pointing. "Pavla Blanca."

The eddy took shape as it neared the summit of the dune; it filled out—it was a woman. Right at the crest she stood erect and bent forward, as if peering into the shadows beyond the hill upon which she stood. Pavla Blanca, the White Wraith, dressed in her flowing wedding gown. She poised for an instant, still looking, then ran along the rippled edge of the dune. She disappeared with a sound that was halfway between a sigh and a sob. Of course it was just the wind. But I decided, from that time on, to leave it to others to refute old Spanish legends.[6]

The real identity of Pavla Blanca was the fiancé of a conquistador. Her name was Mañuela, and the conquistador was Hernando de Luna, one of Francisco de Coronado's men employed in the search for the fabled Seven Cities of Gold. Mañuela remained in Mexico under the agreement that when the northern Kingdom of New Spain was properly settled, de Luna would send for her to join him. Instead, on the trek across the dreaded Jornada del Muerto, Coronado's men were attacked by the Apache. De Luna became separated from the troop and soon found himself lost among the blinding white sands. Coronado and his men traced de Luna's tracks across the dunes but never found his body. It was as though he disappeared into thin air.

(Historical Society for Southeast New Mexico)

Mañuela headed north into the region upon news of her fiancé's disappearance, escorted by a group of Jesuits. One night, under cover of darkness, Mañuela donned her wedding dress, mounted a horse, and rode off into the sands, never to be seen again—not in corporeal form at least. As stated before, now her ghostly essence is seen among the swirling sands carried in the winds.

(Historical Society for Southeast New Mexico)

Either history repeated itself years later, or the tale of Pavla Blanca received an update in modern times. Writer Alice Bullock also related the tale of two young lovers, an Alamogordo teacher and her fiancé, who went for a romantic picnic on the sands one evening before sunset. The man, who was not native to the area, was fascinated by the dunes. After dinner, as his fiancé packed up the picnic baskets, he decided to climb the tallest dune he saw. The teacher watched as a strange wind erased his footsteps from the sand. As she called to him to come back, he was completely obscured by the sandy winds. When they subsided, he was gone, never to be seen again.

Supposedly, search parties scoured the sands only to find nothing.[7] Bullock stated that the teacher herself disappeared into the sands in search of her beloved. She became a woman in white, not unlike La Llorona, as she is glimpsed in her wedding dress, dancing atop the dunes as the white sand swirls around her. Bullock, who heard the tale in a schoolroom setting, concluded her tale,

> A shy little girl told me, softly, she knows where the teacher and her man are – in the Pueblo of the old ones. They will awaken when the Indians do and the white sands roll away. Could be![8]

Chapter Notes

---

[1] Bullock, *Monumental Ghosts* (Kindle Location 363).

[2] Ibid.

[3] Ibid.

[4] Ibid, (Kindle Locations 380-386).

[5] Pavla Blanca basically translates to white dust.

[6] Charles, *Tales of the Tularosa*, pp. 50-51.

[7] Along the same lines, no stories about the incident can be found in newspapers, alluding to this just being an urban legend.

[8] Bullock, *Monumental Ghosts* (Kindle Locations 398-403).

DELVERS FIND GIANT'S BONES

From New Mexico Comes Wondrous Story of a Skeleton.

Special Dispatch to The Call.

EAST LAS VEGAS, N. M., Jan. 19.— An archaeological find has been made on the Mesa Rica, near Chapento, this county. It is the skeleton of a prehistoric man. Legend has it that the vicinity of the Chapento and the Mesa Rica was peopled by a race of giants centuries ago. Evidence to substantiate this tradition was found on the ranch of Don Luciano Quintano.

Five men, several days ago, began to excavate at a place marked by two pieces of rough-hewn white building stone about fifteen feet apart. They had dug about five feet between the stones when the skeleton was unearthed. The bones are well preserved.

The San Francisco Call and Post (January 20, 1902).

6

CEMETERY OF THE GIANTS
Mystery of Mesa Rica

According to Navajo legend, the Hero Twins slew the fearsome giant Yé'iitsoh atop Mount Taylor near Grants. The giant's blood then flowed down the mountain to become the lava flow of the malpais. If there's any truth to the legend, then perhaps the Hero Twins really slew Yé'iitsoh atop Mesa Rica in Guadalupe County, for that is where real giant bones were reported to have been found.

Located north of and just between Santa Rosa and Tucumcari, Mesa Rica is, for the most part, in the middle of nowhere. Back in 1901, Mesa Rica was situated on the land of a rancher named Luciano Quintana.[1] The mesa was regarded as a strange place by the old-timers of Quintana's time. Supposedly, tall tales circulated that it had once been inhabited by giants. As evidence for the story, atop the mesa were stones bearing "curious inscriptions"[2] placed in such a way that they resembled a graveyard. However, they were much too large to be tombstones... unless they marked the burial plot of a giant. Along those same lines, supposedly giant tools and implements too large for any normal human to handle had been found in the area. "Rude implements of enormous size have been found that could not have been used by anyone with strength short of an ox," reported the *White Oaks Eagle* of February 6, 1902.

Quintana had grown up hearing stories of giants in the land since he was a boy. Gathering up five friends, he decided to see if there was any truth to the legends by exhuming one of the gigantic graves in the latter half of January 1902. What they found, if true, was shocking. Per the *White Oaks Eagle*:

> Selecting five others to assist him in the work he picked out two of the largest stones and began to take up the earth between them. The work took several days on account of the obstacles which had been placed in the way.
>
> At a depth of six feet a layer of rock two feet thick had to be taken out. They had evidently been selected according to their shape before being placed in the ground for each one fitted closely to the other.
>
> After disposing of the rock a layer of what had once been wood was taken out three feet in thickness. Another two feet of pure white sand was taken out of the hole and the bones of a man were found.
>
> Though the grave was fifteen feet long and eight feet wide the body had to all appearances been first placed in the hole in a sitting position and then doubled over until the face rested on the feet.
>
> Some of the bones which had withstood the onslaught of decay show the owner to have been one of the largest men that ever lived.
>
> From those found it is calculated that the giant must have been at least seventeen feet high. A forearm found measures nearly four feet, and is in perfect proportion in every other way. Only the lower jaw bone is preserved and is three feet from one end to the other. A tooth which was still sticking in it is as large as a small bucket.
>
> Those who saw the bones say that his chest measurement must have been one hundred and twenty inches. The ribs are enormous and are large enough to withstand a fierce attack with weapons such as these people must have had.

There are numerous other tombstones five feet long in the vicinity that are supposed to be over skeletons of giants. Plans are being laid to dig between all of them and learn whether or not there are more remains to be found.

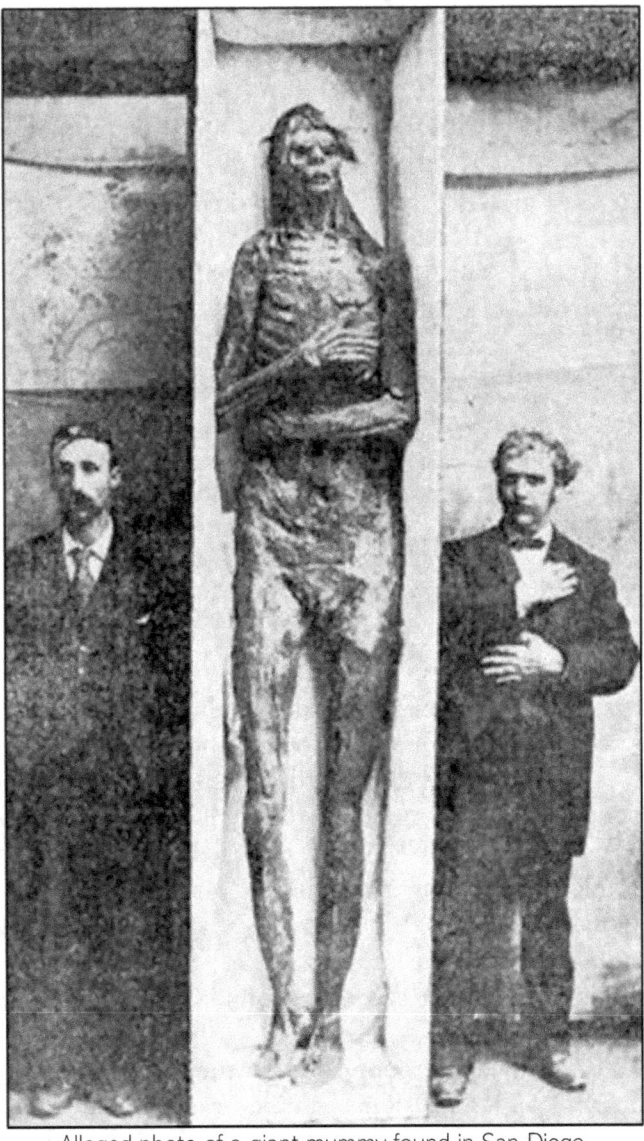

Alleged photo of a giant mummy found in San Diego.

"GIANTS IN THOSE DAYS"
DOWN IN MEXICO.

Skeleton of a Prodigiously Enormous
Human Being Found On a Mesa
Rica Ranch.

East Las Vegas, N. M., Jan. 30.—
Legend has it that the vicinity of Ca-
pento and the Mesa Rica was peopled
by a race of giants centuries ago, and
evidence to substantiate the story has
been found on the ranch of Don Luciano Quintano. Five men several days
ago began to axcavate at a place on his
ranch marked by two pieces of rough-
hewn white building stone about fifteen
feet apart.

They had dug about five feet between
the stones when a skeleton was un-
eathed. It is well preserved. The giant's
chest measurement could have been no
less than eight feet. The lower jaw
bone is all that remains of the head.
It is a massive piece, and in it a huge
tooth. The fore arm measured four feet
and the length of the arm must have
been about eight feet. The skeleton
will be sent to the Archaeological Society at Santa Fe.

The *Charlotte News* of January 13, 1902.

After the exhumation, which seemed to have taken place on January 20th, the *Albuquerque Daily Citizen* of January 27th reported that about a week later, Don Gregorio Varela and Marcello Martinez had ventured to Mesa Rica to try and buy the skeleton from Quintana. If he sold it to them or not is unknown, but the same article, reprinted from the *Las Vegas Optic*, stated that the "skeleton will be on exhibition in the courthouse yard and anthropologists are especially invited to examine it."

The *Leavenworth Weekly Times* of January 23rd reported that "No scientific persons have examined the skeleton and beyond the fact that it is that of a human being, nothing is known." Other papers surmised that the skeleton would be sent to the Archaeological Society at Santa Fe. If they received it, and what they did with it if so, went unreported.

The story made it to the February 11, 1902 edition of the *New York Times* as well, which reported that Quintana had since uncovered many more burial plots that might yield additional giant bones. It also claimed that archeologists were preparing to scour the mesa as well. Again, there were no follow-up articles after this to be found, not on this author's part, at least.

Because many articles appeared on the find, but not on its aftermath, two conclusions can be reached depending on one's mindset. The supernaturally minded may smell a cover-up, while a skeptic might simply say the story was made-up, or that the bones were simply those of a prehistoric animal rather than a "monster man".

Giants Were Buried There

Astounding Story Of A Wonderful Race

GREAT MONOLITHS

Used To Mark the Graves Of Men Who Must Have Been Seventeen Feet In Height.

The El Paso Herald of January 21, 1902.

A Monster of Ye Olden Times.

Santos Lopez came in from Chaperito today and reports the country on the Mesa Rico wild with excitement over the unearthing of the well preserved skeleton of a human giant in that vicinty. Tradition had long whispered of the burial of such a monster in that country and Luciana Quintana organized a party of five persons to locate it. They found it on the premises of Quintana's ranch, the great grave being marked at the head and foot by roughly hewn building stone. The grave was 15 feet long and 8 feet in width. The body had been broken in order to get it into the grave which was too short.

The forearm, from wrist to elbow, measures four feet. The jaw bone is a good three feet. Only the lower jaw bone is preserved. In it is a tooth large enough for a milk stool. The ribs are enormous. The five men who saw the grave opened and who measured the dead giant agreed that his chest measurement could not have been less than eight feet. Other rough tombstones in that vicinity indicate that thereabout sleep other remnants of a race without a name and without a history written only in the bowels of the silent earth.—Las Vegas Optic.

As it stands, the Mesa Rica formation that runs through New Mexico, Colorado, and Oklahoma is peppered with dinosaur bones. However, no indigenous peoples would have taken the time and care to bury the bones if they were those of a long-dead dinosaur or other large prehistoric animal.[3] As it was, the Navajo and many other Native American tribes were loath to touch the bones of the dead lest they rile up a spirit. The headstones and the burials would seem to imply the gigantic bones were buried by humans. As such, if the story is true, the odds would favor the idea of a giant being buried by a giant as opposed to prehistoric peoples burying the bones of a prehistoric animal.

Chapter Notes

[1] While it doesn't prove that he found a giant, Quintana appeared in the papers frequently enough to prove that he at least was a real person and not a "character" invented for the story.

[2] "Giant Skeletons Found," *New York Times* (February 11, 1902).

[3] *The Optic* at one point described the remains with the made-up word "mastodonic," though they seemed to be using it to describe the size, not to imply that it was a mastodon.

Low Falls

Aquellos dos Pilomillos

Tres Stumps

Ruins of Cabin
GOLD IS BURIED HERE

"Secret Door"

MALPAIS

The Pumpkin Patch

Sno-Ta-Hay Canyon

ALSO CALLED Z CANYON, ZIG ZAG CANYON, GOLD CANYON, ADAMS DIGGINGS CANYON & HIDDEN BOX CANYON, AS DESCRIBED BY SURVIVORS OF APACHE ATTACK.

7

THE LOST ADAMS DIGGINGS
Secret of Sno-Ta-Hay Canyon

Of all the yarns that vied for the title of New Mexico's greatest treasure story, the Lost Adams Diggings was once the grandest of them all. Though it has since been eclipsed by the likes of Victorio Peak, in its day, the story of the lost canyon of gold reigned supreme in saloons across the Southwest. The tale had been told countless times during the Old West, but it was Texas folklorist J. Frank Dobie who brought the Lost Adams into the 20th century, serving as the centerpiece for Dobie's book *Apache Gold & Yaqui Silver*.

However, there were so many varying versions of the story that Dobie had to settle on a pastiche. For instance, sometimes the gold was hidden among the malpais south of Grants. Other times, the diggings were discovered in the Datil Mountains, or in the Plains of San Augustin near Socorro. It was even speculated to reside as far north as the Navajo country near Gallup. So many differing versions were given of the terrain and its landmarks, that all anyone could really do was triangulate the basic region of the lost diggings. This triangle extended between two points in New Mexico and one in Arizona, those being from Silver City, to Grants, and then to Alpine, Arizona.

The nebulous location of the gold aside, the basic story centered around a man known only as Adams. In August of 1864, Adams had been running freight between Tucson and Los Angeles when he found himself stranded in the Arizona desert after an Indian raid. Making his way to a friendly Pima village, Adams fell in with a group of twenty or so prospectors in the process of being led to a canyon of gold by a half-breed Indian they called Gotch Ear.

California 49ers on the trail of the Gold Rush.

The group set out in a northeasterly direction towards two mysterious peaks, which Gotch Ear claimed the canyon was about six days from. Eventually the group came upon a bluff, and blending into it was a large boulder that served as a secret door into the canyon. The passageway was unique in the way that it literally zigzagged in the shape of a gigantic Z. When the party entered the canyon, they found it to be an oasis of trees with a large cascading waterfall that produced a clear running stream. And in that stream was gold. Lots and lots of gold.

In his 1919 pamphlet, "The Adams Gold Diggings," W.H. Byerts claimed that "the gold mines of Solomon, the Klondike or Africa" couldn't be compared to the diggings. As for the canyon itself, Adams per Byerts said that it was "hemmed in by perpendicular rocks hundreds of feet high as far as we could see in every direction, and our guide told us this canyon was miles long…" Likewise, in his 1935 pamphlet, "The Adams Diggings Story," Charles Allen claimed that the canyon was "about three hundred yards in width" with "a flat bottom, no trees growing in it, but its sides are covered with pines, rather small, about the right size for log cabins."

Another vintage depiction of the California Gold Rush.

As alluded to earlier, in addition to steep cliff walls, the canyon was said to boast a huge waterfall, which was unusual for New Mexico. The grandest description of the waterfall came courtesy of an 1897 account published in the *Socorro Chieftain* from R.C. Patterson, who claimed to have gotten the description from Adams himself: "The water in this valley ran northwest and at the lower end fell over a precipice eighty feet high."[1]

For a time, the miners inhabited the paradise-like canyon in peace, panning the golden sands of the stream from sunrise to sundown. When it was determined that they could potentially occupy the canyon for quite a while, it was decided to build a cabin, under the hearth of which would be hidden the gold. But all good things must come to an end. One day, along came Chief Nana and his Apache warriors. Nana told the prospectors they were welcome to stay in what he called Sno-Ta-Hay Canyon so long as they didn't venture beyond the waterfall.

As you can guess, one of the miners did just that. Above the falls, the miner found an even greater abundance of gold, returning with a nugget as large as a goose egg. Nana and his Apache found out and soon returned to massacre the entire camp. The only survivor was Adams and a lone companion that varied from tale to tale. Though a fortune in gold had been stashed beneath the cabin, Adams only escaped with the large nugget found beyond the falls. Adams made it back to Los Angeles, where he stayed for several years before returning to New Mexico in the 1870s in the company of a backer named Captain Shaw. For the next decade, Adams tried and failed to rediscover the canyon until he met his end in 1886.

Of course, Adams wasn't the only man to stumble across the canyon. An ex-soldier named Jason Baxter claimed to have found it as well in the mid-1870s, as did a German by the name of Jake Schaeffer. In the year 1872, Schaeffer was hired as a cook for a group of soldiers patrolling the Deming region along the Mimbres River. On a hunting excursion, Schaeffer became separated from the main group. He turned up many days later at Fort Craig near Socorro, having wandered hundreds of miles. He was stark naked and out of his mind. All that he carried was a sack of gold nuggets weighing nearly ten pounds. Later, as his sanity slowly returned, he couldn't remember where he had found the gold, only that he had passed a mysterious mountain with the face of a woman painted on it. Like Adams, Schaeffer spent the rest of his days trying and failing to retrace his steps.

Lady Magdalena, Near Magdalena, N. M.

Copyright by W. M. Borrowdale.

The Lady of Magdelena, pictured above, is one of the more famous landmarks in the Socorro region, as it has the profile of a woman's face clearly visible on the side of the mountain. A group of Spanish conquistadors fleeing from the Apache sought refuge under the mountain and claimed that the face appeared and frightened away their pursuers. Local legend had it that the Apache revered the mountain and would not harm anyone who sought solace at its base.

Baxter heard the collective tales of Adams and Schaeffer, and using both, estimated the general area of the diggings. As a starting point, Baxter figured the mountain with the woman's face on it seen by Schaeffer was likely the Lady of Magdalena. Baxter and a companion set out in the vicinity of the Lady of Magdalena and passed it by on their way to the diggings. Baxter and his friend then came across an even more fantastic landmark that he called Island Mountain. Interestingly, Baxter likened it to the ruins of an ancient civilization, stating that it brought to mind the pyramids of Egypt. "As I neared the Island Mountain the plants got weird," Baxter remembered. He elaborated that there "were immense sotols and the largest cacti I have ever seen" in the area as well. "I could see mirages off to the east, and once in a while a salt laguna."[2]

As Baxter's luck would have it, his mule actually wandered right to the secret door of Sno-Ta-Hay Canyon. Baxter and his companion followed it inside, seeing many signs of former habitation. Since some signs implied a former Anglo presence, Baxter knew this had to be the canyon discovered by Adams and Schaeffer. "The water increased as we went up and the canyon walls of white quartz became tinted like a rainbow in the evenin' air," Baxter remembered. "All the clays and rocks looked mineralized."[3]

Baxter and his companion spent the rest of the day prospecting. However, before they knew it, it was nearing dark, and storm clouds were brewing, so Baxter and his partner made camp for the night. In a story even more exciting than Adams', in the darkness, the Apache attacked. Amidst a thundering rainstorm that nearly flooded the canyon, Baxter and his companion fled with the Apache hot on their trail. The duo escaped with their lives, and in the 1880s, Baxter recruited a friend named James McKenna to search out the canyon with him. What Baxter and McKenna found was quite discouraging. When returning to the spot of the canyon, the area appeared to have been decimated in an earthquake.

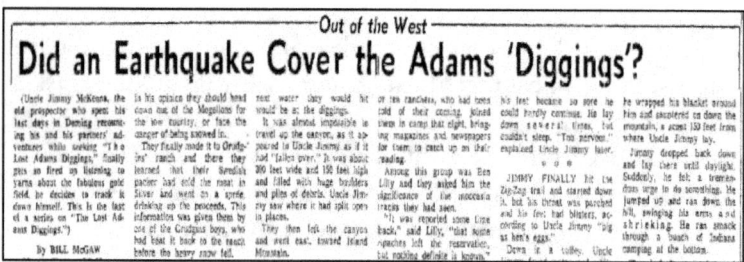

The *El Paso Herald Post* of February 17, 1962.

The first casualty was Island Mountain. McKenna related:

> Baxter rode ahead to look for the opening into the park. When we came up we found him staring around him like one in a daze. And no wonder! The whole mountain looked as if it had been crushed by giant hands, as a child would crush a snowball. Even the ridge was broken in many places. Not a sign of a tree or an animal could be seen in any direction. Immense

boulders lay tumbled together as if they had crashed in a mighty battle, scattering splinters in every direction. Following the broken ridge we came to the spot where Baxter expected to find the opening to the park. Instead of the park we came into a barren gulch filled in places almost to the top with rocks and debris. No water. No vegetation. No animals. No mineral.

"This sure beats hell!" was all Baxter could find to say. We went along the sides of the gulch looking for a level stretch to camp, but there was none. "This mountain looks as if it had busted open in a big explosion," said Poland, and it was all that was said by any of us as we climbed over the rocks and the debris.[4]

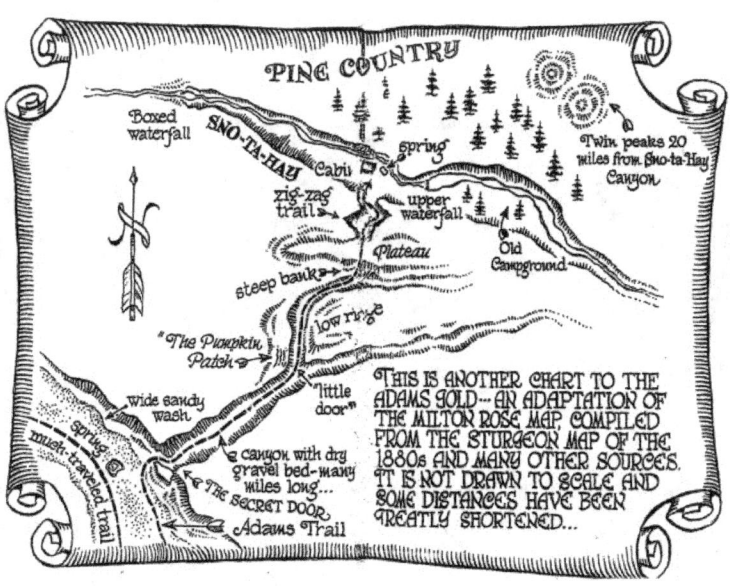

A bit later, when looking for another landmark that Baxter identified as Pink Hill, Baxter theorized, "From what I see the Lost Diggin's are now in a Lost Canyon, scattered more likely to the head of the Little Colorado River."[5] Baxter continued,

"It seems to me that first there came a quake which pretty near shook the mountain to pieces, and then cloudburst that carried away whatever gold or mineral was in the canyon. Even the rocks look strange, mostly a burnt out lava and a species of diorite. The Pink Hill may have been a volcanic vent, producing gold. The mineral zone must have been small or we'd be able to find extensions nearby, but you can see for yourselves there's nothing here but lava, or malpais. In time someone may locate a valuable copper mine in the canyon with the blue-stained shale, but it's not for us."[6]

According to the Apache spiritual belief, gold nuggets could be picked up from the ground if the earth had already yielded them. However, digging gold from the earth itself was another matter. If man dug too deeply into the earth, the Apache creator God, Ussen, would send an earthquake. Perhaps this is why the Apache despised the unearthing of gold in Sno-Ta-Hay Canyon. Had the prospectors dug deeply into the ground, then a great earthquake would have befallen all of Apacheria. The daughter of the Apache leader Perico, Darlene Enjady, explained to Eve Ball, "You can pick it up off the ground, but you mustn't dig for it because the Mountain Spirits would get mad and make an earthquake."[7] (Apache Spirit Dancers as photographed by Katherine Taylor Dodge c. 1899.)

"Boys, we sure came to Lost Canyon Diggins," Baxter said. "There'll never be any yellow nuggets found here unless there comes another earthquake and cloudburst to throw and wash back into the gulch what they took out of it."[8] Baxter then suggested that perhaps next spring they could return and see if the landscape had been altered further in a positive way instead of a negative one.

Charles Allen was also of the opinion that Adams believed the landscape of the canyon had irrevocably been changed due to weather. Allen wrote, "Adams was of the opinion that a waterspout had washed trees, boulders, and rubbish to the box canyon, choking it and filling the canyon above the dam so formed with debris."[9]

Likewise, the *Socorro Chieftain* of January 9, 1904, wrote of the diggings that "Any mountainous country is subject to great changes in the lapse of years, and it is probable that all traces of the original workings are covered deep with soil from the wash of the surrounding hills."

All things considered, it seems that either an earthquake, a deluge, or a combination of the two have truly turned the Lost Adams Diggings into a lost world.

Chapter Notes

---

[1] Any native New Mexican can tell you there are certainly no eighty-foot waterfalls here.
[2] McKenna, *Black Range Tales*, p.44.
[3] Ibid.
[4] Ibid, p.62.
[5] Ibid.
[6] Ibid, p.63.
[7] Robinson, *Apache Voices*, p.110.
[8] McKenna, *Black Range Tales*, p.63.

8

VILLAGE OF THE WITCHES
Los Voladeros, the Flyers

In addition to many other things, New Mexico was also once a land of witchcraft and witches. But these weren't your typical broomstick-riding, black-cat-petting witches. In fact, New Mexico witches, called *brujas*, didn't even ride brooms. If they rode anything, they might have ridden a pumpkin or an egg, but typically they turned into owls or fireballs to take flight. As such, they were sometimes also called *los voladeros*, or the flyers. Whether they could actually fly or not, almost all New Mexico villages had their own verifiable witches. The famous New Mexico explorer Charles Lummis even photographed three witches in San Rafael, and one of them appeared to be giving his camera the Evil Eye.

While all villages had their witches, whether real or imagined, it was whispered that somewhere high in the mountains of New Mexico existed a hidden colony comprised of nothing but witches. It was called Los Voladeros and resided on the highest peak in the vicinity of Truchas and Mora. According to modern-day folklorist Ray John de Aragón, Los Voladeros was a virtual citadel, hidden behind a fortress-like wall high "up in the clouds surrounded by mountains at the highest point near Mora."[1]

In *Enchanted Legends and Lore of New Mexico*, Aragón told of a young man who had a burning curiosity to visit the forbidden village that his elders warned him of. So, despite their warnings, one day he saddled up his horse and set off into the mountains to find the mysterious settlement. He arrived at the crest of the mountaintop at nightfall and could no longer see well. He thought back to what the elders had warned of. They said that if one approached the village in the dark, they would only need to look for a narrow, moonlit path. Whatever happened, one was not to stray from the path, as that would mean death. Lastly, one would know they were nearing the village upon hearing the hooting of many owls.

With an elevation of just a little over 13,000 feet, Truchas Peak among the Sangre De Cristo Mountains is the most likely candidate for Ray John de Aragón's version of Los Voladeros.

Just as the elders said, the man followed the forested path until he heard the hooting of the owls and could see the embers of fires floating into the air from fireplaces. The village was near, obscured behind a fortress-like wall. The man crept along the wall until he found an opening and snuck through into the forbidden village. At once, he was struck by a type of magic and fell to the ground unconscious.

When he awoke, he found himself imprisoned within a torreon, or circular adobe tower. However, the stay wasn't all bad. He was well fed with delicious food from a beautiful female jailer. Actually, when the young man was finally released, he realized that the entire village was populated exclusively by beautiful women. However, all of them wore black dresses and black shawls as though they were in mourning.

"The Three Witches" of San Rafael as photographed by Charles Lummis.

Eventually, the young man fell in love with his beautiful jailer and asked her to marry him. She agreed, and on the wedding day, rather than white, she wore a black dress and a black shawl embroidered with black roses. At the wedding ceremony, for the first time, a man in the form of the priest performing the ceremony appeared. However, he had an odd resemblance to the Devil, with his upturned eyebrows, goatee, and pointed ears.

After this, the young man returned to his old village with his new wife and also his mother-in-law. That's when the young man finally began to notice how strange the duo were. Sometimes he could smell sulfur in their presence, and he noticed they disappeared every night as well. Thinking his wife was having an affair, one night he crept to the door and peered outside when she left. His beautiful wife had turned into an old hag. In an instant, she and her mother transformed into owls and took flight. The young man finally realized he had married a witch. Not knowing what else to do, he burned all of his wife's bewitched possessions outside and then barricaded himself in the house.

Locked out of the house, the two witches tormented the young man in their owl forms until he finally went crazy. The villagers had known all along though. Not only had they warned him not to go to Los Voladeros, but they had watched him return with an old hag who had bewitched him into thinking she was a beautiful woman. While the story was obviously a folktale, there might have been a real village called Los Voladeros that influenced it.

In addition to the mystical Los Voladeros, there were other villages considered to be the headquarters of all the witches in New Mexico. One account told of two men perched atop a ridge witnessing fireballs rising from every house in Valdez village, shown above. The fireballs were witches in flight on their way to the Witches Sabbat.

Author Nasario García interviewed a man who indicated Los Voladeros was a real place in his book *Tales of Witchcraft and the Supernatural in the Pecos Valley*. The informant was Pablo Aguilar, born in 1913. Aguilar recounted an incident from his youth when he traveled with his mother and brother on horseback from Villanueva to La Pintada, another village fifty some miles away to the south. Because of the long distance, they had gotten up very early in the morning to hit the trail. In particular, there was a steep slope they had to climb on their way there along the Villanueva trail. Apparently, Los Voladeros was located somewhere in that vicinity.[2] In Aguilar's own words, "When we got to the foot of the trail, Mom looked on up ahead, up towards a place called Los Voladeros. Way up at the peak of the tallest of Los Voladeros, there was this little old lady like so [hunched up], at about five, six o'clock in the morning."[3]

Becoming frightened at the sight of what was surely a witch near the main witch village itself, Aguilar's mother urged her children to hurry up the hill and not look at the old woman. Aguilar noted that the horse he was riding was usually notoriously slow and stubborn when it came to climbing steep trails; but not that day. That day the horse made great haste, and the trio made it to La Pintada in record time, arriving there by two in the afternoon. When Aguilar's mother told her father of the incident upon arriving there, he told her that it was indeed a witch they saw.

Even if there's not much to that particular story, it does indicate that there was a belief in a real village of witches called Los Voladeros. And, though you can call Aguilar superstitious if you want, you have to wonder why such an old woman would be hanging out alone on a high mountain peak before dawn. Perhaps she was simply there to watch the sunrise. Or, maybe she was a witch winding down from her nightly prowl...

Chapter Notes

[1] Aragón, *Enchanted Legends and Lore*, p.23.
[2] Due to the discrepancies in the locations between Aragón's version of Los Voladeros and Aguilar's, it's possible that the name Los Voladeros was ascribed to several different mountains of New Mexico.
[3] García, *Tales of Witchcraft*, p.25.

9
HOLY MISSION CITY
Socorro's Forgotten Settlement

I n Socorro once lived a mining engineer by the name of W.H. Byerts. Historically speaking, he's probably best remembered as the author of one of the first major works outlining the Lost Adams Diggings. His pamphlet, published in 1919, provided most of the foundation for J. Frank Dobie's writings on the subject. Prior to popularizing the Lost Adams Diggings, Byerts, in an attempt to drum up interest in a mining venture, apparently dreamed up an entirely fictitious tale involving a lost Spanish mission. Printed in *The Mexican Mining Journal* of September 1912, Byerts told of something he called the Iron Door Mine, said to have been lost during the Pueblo Revolt of 1680.

Byerts' account seemed to be copied from numerous other "lost padre mine" stories common to the Southwest, wherein Catholic priests induced Indian slave labor to mine a rich vein. Byerts placed the mine in Socorro's Blue Canyon, south of Socorro Peak. Byerts wrote,

> The location was selected primarily because of the large spring of pure warm water which gushes out of the rock at the base of the Socorro mountains, three miles to the west of the Rio Grande river bottoms. The city was founded by catholic monks and called the Holy Mission City.

HISTORY AND LEGEND OF THE IRON DOOR PROPERTY.

Written for the Mexican Mining Journal.

By W. H. Byerts. *

Though there was certainly a mission in Socorro at the time, as far as history goes it was known as Nuestra Señora de Perpetuo Socorro, the first Catholic mission which was established in the area in 1626. However, according to the account of Byerts, Mission City was begotten by area Jesuits and the adjoining mine began operating in 1585, prior to the building of Nuestra Señora de Perpetuo Socorro.

Socorro's San Miguel Church as depicted by Confederate soldier Albert Peticolas on February 26, 1864, while passing through Socorro after the Battle of Valverde.

Byerts went on to describe the paradise that was Holy Mission City:

This beautiful valley with its fertile soils, producing wonderful fruits and champaign grapes soon became a vast garden, the monks importing the choicest fruits and grapes from Europe to which the soil was well adapted. While wonderful progress was being made in agriculture and horticulture, the mines in the Blue canyon, three and a half miles to the west of the Mission City were being opened up and their production was increasing yearly. The amount of gold and silver bullion that was annually exported to Europe amounted to millions of dollars and Mission City became famous through its wonderful mineral production.

Life at Holy Mission City, which Byerts said was the "largest and wealthiest [city] in the southwest," revolved around the Iron Door Mine, so named because the "mine had but one opening, through a tunnel, which was closed with a heavy iron door from which the property derived its name."

Socorro Peak as depicted on an old postcard.

For nearly one hundred years, the mine produced until 1684—four years after the Spanish were expelled. (Obviously, Byerts only had a loose handle on the dates.) Byerts claimed that millions of dollars' worth of gold ore was mined and sent to Europe. What wasn't sent back to Spain was kept at the mines, where gold and silversmiths spent their days hammering the precious metals into jewelry. "A golden chandelier, suspended from the ceiling by heavy silver chains, together with fascinating altar ornaments of gold and silver, attested to the tremendous wealth of the Iron Door property," Byerts claimed, and also said that the mission there was "the wealthiest in the country at that time." As such, Mission City then went on to become renowned across the Southwest.

It all came to an end with a massive earthquake which struck in the year 1684—also the year of the Pueblo Revolt according to Byerts. Sounding like something out of a Cecil B. DeMille epic, Byerts said that "an earthquake of tremendous force broke off an overhanging ledge on Socorro Peak, flinging millions of tons of rock downward, completely burying the portal of the Iron Door Mine and trapping 500 miners." While the Spaniards worked hard to free the trapped miners, the Indians took advantage of the situation and revolted. The Indians then drove every last Spaniard from New Spain and then proceeded to destroy all traces of the mine and Mission City. Byerts wrote,

> Every vestige of this early civilization and immense wealth was wiped out; the church alone remaining, a monument to that which had gone before. All traces of the mines and city were destroyed during this time and not until the year 1880 was there another mining venture promoted.

It's debatable where Byerts' tale came from. It's entirely possible that Byerts collected a hodgepodge of conflicting accounts and then cobbled them into a romantic pastiche. Or, maybe it was entirely made up. Writer Den Galbraith covered the story in *Frontier Times* in 1964 and theorized that Byerts likely "got his story from the 'archives' of some old-timer's mind, recapitulated around a campfire, aided and abetted by a jug of 'Taos Lightning.'"[1]

Desert scene from Socorro County, New Mexico.

Galbraith continued that "W.H. Byerts willfully succumbed to a wild dream, which he pieced together from many sources—Indians, Mexicans, and all the old-timers he could talk to."[2] While it's true that evidence of Spanish mining could be found across Socorro County, Galbraith asserted that Byerts' engineered the theory of the Iron Door Mine to help promote the then-current Iron Door Mines of the Socorro Region. In his article, Byerts reported that

At this time a number of claims were located including the Torrence and Merrit, Morning Star and others. The Torrence and Merrit were worked from 1880 to 1885 and produced over a million dollars worth of bullion and the deepest workings did not go down over 150 feet, only the surface deposits being worked. All of these properties have been purchased by one company together with the location where the famous Iron Door property was located and are again known as the Iron Door Mines of Socorro. At the present time a tunnel is being driven under the old workings from the base of the mountain, which will open up the mine at a depth of 500 feet. The tunnel is now in over 500 feet and is being pushed day and night with every expectation of opening up one of the great gold-silver deposits of the southwest.

Byerts' fluff piece worked, and he secured several new investors in his venture. The New Mexico Bureau of Mines reported in their No.8 Bulletin in 1913 that "Byerts Tunnel" was bored into Socorro Peak at a depth of 1,280 feet. It found nothing. And nor did the historical record support the existence of anything so grand as Holy Mission City in the vicinity of Socorro. As such, the fantastic lost city of gold was just as mythical as those searched for by Coronado.

Chapter Notes

[1] Galbraith, "Iron Door Mine of Blue Canyon," *Frontier Times* (Sep/Oct 1964) p.53.
[2] Ibid, p.41.

10

MIRAGE CITY OF THE MALPAIS
Phantom Ruins and Cliff Dwellings

E l Malpais National Monument is situated in Cibola County in western New Mexico. For long stretches, fire-blackened lava dominates the scarred landscape.[1] It was created over 200,000 years ago when Mount Taylor erupted. As Jack Kutz elegantly put it in *More Mysteries & Miracles of New Mexico*, "The tortured landscape clearly shows how the unstoppable tide of gushing rock rolled like an ocean wave onto a beach from which it never rolled back."[2]

Navajo legend says the lava flow was the blood of the giant Yé'iitsoh, slain atop Mount Taylor by the Hero Twins. The peoples of Acoma, on the other hand, claimed the black charred earth was created when the Hero Twins confronted the monstrous Kau Bat. When they tore out his eyes, from them spewed the lava-like blood, charring the land in his death throes.

The Anglos and the Spaniards added their legends to the land, too. Pre-conquest, the Spaniards thought it to be the site of gold like everywhere else. Then, during the Pueblo Revolt, stories spread that the Spaniards hid gold in the malpais when they fled New Mexico. Anglos told tales of the local ice caves housing frozen bodies. One had a couple of soldiers from Fort Wingate becoming frozen, and another, a red-bearded outlaw from Arizona.[3]

Oddly enough, beneath the obsidian sea, ice caves can be found. Ironically, what was previously smoldering hot before it cooled and hardened now insulates the ice caves, keeping them frozen year-round, even in the heat of summer. Above is pictured Dave Candelaria, owner of the land housing both the ice caves and Bandera Crater, exploring a small ice cave. (*Albuquerque Journal*, October 14, 1955)

The most fantastic legend of the malpais is easily that of the ghostly White Pueblo, though. It can only be seen at sundown; it cannot be glimpsed again anytime else. Though several witnesses attested to seeing the striking white pueblo jutting from out of the black lava rock, all attempts to actually locate it always failed.

Unfortunately, no detailed accounts exist of the cliff dwellings alleged to exist among the malpais, but they likely resemble Montezuma Castle of Arizona, pictured above (c.1897 by Edgar A. Mearns).

A.J. Atkinson, a writer for *Gold!* magazine, went to Acoma to ferret out the folklore behind this strange legend in 1997. An Acoma man related to him a story not dissimilar to the disappearing pueblo of White Sands. The Acoma man said that in ancient times, there had been a small tribe of peaceful people. To escape the dangers of other war-like tribes, they sought solace in the inhospitable malpais. There, they built a pueblo, and their shaman placed a spell on the settlement so that it would be invisible to all but its residents. Atkinson even chartered a plane to fly over the malpais to see if there was any truth to the story, but saw nothing.

Long before that, the *Albuquerque Journal* of October 14, 1955, recounted a similar legend, writing how "a peaceful people once inhabited the mesas and plains which surround the lava flow." It continued that

They were farmers who lived in the now ruined pueblos. As time went on a warlike tribe began to prey on the pueblo dwellers, killing off the men, destroying the crops and stealing the girls and women. Finally, in desperation the peacelovers constructed a pueblo of white rock in the midst of the lava, a place that afforded little opportunity for agriculture, but wonderful natural defenses.

What became of these people is one of the secrets of New Mexico.

An old-timer from Grants also told the paper,

"Sure [the White Pueblo is] there, but it's enchanted. You have to believe if you are to find it, then someday you'll stumble right on the place. I know three men who have found it while herding sheep. That was a long time ago and they're all dead now."

Postcard showing the ice cave near Bandera Crater.

Dave Candelaria, who owned the land on which Bandera Crater and its fantastic ice caves were located, sought out the truth of the legend.[4] And, if anyone could have found the White Pueblo, it would have been Candelaria. During his explorations, Candelaria found everything from Native American pottery to abandoned whiskey stills from the Prohibition Era.

"Thus far Candelaria has located nothing that resembles a pueblo ruin, white or otherwise," the *Journal* wrote, then added, "But he continues to search at every opportunity, for he feels certain that such a place does exist."

Beloved New Mexico writer Howard Bryan naturally gave the white pueblo a passing mention in an article he did on the malpais for the *Albuquerque Tribune* on May 3, 1969:

ACCORDING TO ONE old legend, there is a prehistoric Indian pueblo, built of white sandstone rock, hidden in the center of the lava beds. No trace of this abandoned pueblo has ever been found, or spotted from the air, but the legend lives on.

As surprising as this might sound, it's possible that tales of the White Pueblo were based upon more grounded accounts of cliff-dwelling ruins in a hidden canyon in the malpais. Alvin D. Hudson, a Texas-based turquoise dealer, gave an in-depth account of the ancient ruins of the malpais in the *El Paso Herald* of August 6, 1927. In it, Hudson told of a Puebloan whose father had been an Indian scout in the 1870s and 1880s. "When Hudson's friend was only a boy his father used to tell him of a wonderful lost city he had seen on one of his scouting expeditions [into the malpais]," the *Herald* reported.[5]

The article continued that the scout had just endured an arduous trek across the malpais when he came upon "the north bank of a deep box canyon just after sunset."[6] The scout camped there for the night and saw the "lost city" the next morning just before sunrise:

He was looking down into the canyon when on one of the canyon walls he saw a large group of cliff dwellings under a protecting cliff. Even as he watched the sun began to rise and as the long shadows shot across the canyon and blotted out the city before his very eyes.

Evidently the only time the city could be seen from any distance was just before sunrise, the old scout said.[7]

Ruins near Fort Wingate, not far from Grants, New Mexico.

The old government scout made a subsequent trip into the malpais again thirty years later and returned home with gold nuggets and pieces of turquoise. Just before he died in 1896, he told his son he had found the gold in the same canyon as the lost city.

Old postcard depicting the malpais created by Mt. Taylor.

Hudson also had an archeologist friend, C.B. Wilson of El Paso, who was taken to the city by an Indian guide in 1918. Initially, Wilson was told by another Indian friend that if he wanted to "see something that few white men had ever seen" there was a man at Laguna Pueblo who could take him to a "lost city." The Laguna man, so Wilson was told, had been following a wounded deer one day when he suddenly found himself in front of a wonderful city akin to an old Spanish mission. A solid gold bell hung from its tower, and inside the mission, images of hammered gold were on the altar—or so the guide said.

Eventually, Wilson took the unnamed Laguna man up on his offer. Over the course of four days, Wilson was led through the treacherous malpais to the canyon. Wilson and his guide approached via the north rim of the canyon wall and descended by rope. As promised, the ruins were there. However, according to Hudson, Wilson had taken along a camera into the canyon. Presumably, he would have photographed the ruins, but so far, no photos of them have ever emerged. Perhaps they reside in a dusty old attic somewhere. Or, perhaps the story was made up altogether. Real or not, could these hidden ruins have been the basis for the legend of the White Pueblo? Or are they just another enigma hidden within the lava fields?

Chapter Notes

---

[1] In fact, the lands were so charred that the U.S. Army considered the malpais as a testing ground for the first A-Bomb since the land was burnt already.

[2] Kutz, *More Mysteries & Miracles of New Mexico*, p.53.

[3] The frozen soldiers were reported to the Forest Service in Albuquerque by a hiker in the 1950s. Not yet a national monument, the malpais were out of the Forest Service's jurisdiction, so the story was never officially investigated. The tale of the frozen outlaw came from H.W. Stowell, who said an Indian friend took him to explore the ice caves in the 1930s.

[4] The Candelarias, it should be noted, were legend among New Mexico tourism, working tirelessly to get roads into the harsh badlands to promote the fantastic ice caves.

[5] "EL PASOAN HAS OLD MAP TO MUCH SOUGHT PLACER," *El Paso Herald* (August 6, 1927).

[6] Ibid.

[7] Ibid.

11

RUINS OF GRAN QUIVIRA
Lost Capital of New Spain

Situated smack dab in the middle of New Mexico near Socorro, Gran Quivira is just off the southeastern slope of the Chupadera Mesa. And though Gran Quivira is easily accessible today as a state monument, for a time, newspapers sensationalized it as a lost civilization. For early day pioneers, the mysterious ruins were the source of much speculation. Some thought it was merely another abandoned settlement left behind in the Pueblo Revolt of 1680, while others ascribed to it a legend befitting Atlantis. Along these lines, some blamed an earthquake for its destruction. Others thought the gushing lava flow from Little Black Peak, which created the malpais of Carrizozo, caused its desertion.

At its peak, Gran Quivira was thought to have housed between 1,500-3,000 Jumano peoples. Earliest inhabitation was estimated to have begun at around 800 A.D. via construction of pit houses. It was most prominent between the years 1000-1600 A.D. when it served as a trading hub for the Pueblo peoples. Don Juan de Oñate called it Las Humanas when he discovered it in 1598 and claimed it as part of New Spain. By 1629, it was integrated into the Salinas Missions, serving as what was called a *visita*, or a satellite mission sans a permanent priest. That same year, under the supervision of Fray Francisco Letrado, construction on a permanent mission, Iglesia de San Isidro, began and was completed in 1635. However, a combined set of challenges led to the mission's abandonment, chief among them Apache raids along with disease, drought, and famine. By 1678, the Salinas Missions had been completely abandoned. Perhaps it was just as well, for two years later would occur the great Pueblo Revolt, and it would have been vacated anyway.

View of the Gran Quivira ruins. Like any lost city worth its salt, Gran Quivira had a lost treasure associated with it. The *Alamogordo News* of June 13, 1929, reported

Legend has it that about 1680 when the Piros with a few Spaniards were leaving the Gran Quivira, one of the heavy ox wagons which carried 30 burro loads of bullion, about 3,000 pounds, and a small box of diamonds and other precious stones, was surrounded by Apaches above Mesilla in the Rio Grande valley. The Spaniards turned back into the pass of the Organ mountains, and after traveling two days eastward were overtaken by the Indians on the west slope of the mountains believed to be the Sacramentos. The Spaniards, realizing that they were caught, hid the bullion and stones in the soft mud of the cienega. Then they tried to escape and all of them were killed during a running fight along the top of the ridge. Only a boy lived to tell the story. The wagon was deserted about a mile from the place the treasure was buried according to the legend. The boy evaded the Indians and told the story to his mother. From time to time since then, men who claim to be descendants of that family have sought the buried gold. The last visit of these relatives was less than a year ago.

The ruins were rediscovered in 1774 when John Rowzée Peyton, a Virginian traveling up the Rio Grande Valley, stumbled across them. Later, in the aftermath of the Mexican-American War, Anglo settlers began to take note of the ruins. In the absence of known facts, speculative folklore ran wild as pioneers pondered the origins of these fantastic remains. The *Santa Fe New Mexican* of July 19, 1899, for instance, thought that the settlement was "the seat of government of New Spain, where all the wealth of the country was then brought and teemed in treasure vaults of church and state…" As to why Gran Quivira was deserted, a few were well-educated enough to assume that the settlement was abandoned during the Pueblo Revolt. But, others dreamed up more romantic reasons for its desertion.

This letter, published in *The Las Vegas Gazette* of September 23, 1880, was of the opinion that the lava flow from Little Black Peak expelled the people of Gran Quivira. The writer stated that it was his opinion that the peoples of Gran Quivira were "all destroyed, either by the boiling water or the intense heat emanating therefrom, and none were left to tell the story of the terrible catastrophe."

This theory seemed to be popular in 1880. Earlier that year, even Billy the Kid and one of his pals, a cow-puncher by the name of John Meadows, were of the opinion that the area had suffered an earthquake. In the spring of 1880, when the Apache raids were at their height, the duo were on the trail of some missing horses. They had given up on the horses and were looking for water when they came across the ruins of Gran Quivira.[1]

Meadows recollected the following:

> There was a big house at Gran Quivira, in a rather bad state of ruin. It had a cross made of cedar poles on top. We got up on the wall and looked at the cross. I suggested that we take the cross down and examine it but the Kid said: "No, John, it has a history and we'll leave some scientific devil do that."
>
> We had never heard of the old mission at Gran Quivira and it excited our curiosity and interest. What at first appeared to be an old trail leading to the valley to the south, on closer examination proved to be an old irrigation ditch. We took our butcher knives and dug into the bank of the old ditch and found it to be caliche, or deposits of lime made by running water. The ancients must have had sources of water that are not known at present.
>
> What dried up the vegetation, making habitation impossible? I cannot imagine and we could not at that day when Billy the Kid and I camped at Gran Quivira overnight after stolen horses. Neither have I ever heard a reasonable theory advanced that can be substantiated by any known facts. So I will make a guess which ought to be as good as the next one. I believe that earthquakes diverted the surface springs and streams underground many ages ago.[2]

Meadow's theory may have been correct. As it turns out, old Spanish maps indicated a river there that no longer existed. The *Santa Fe New Mexican* of December 27, 1893, noted that "Old Spanish maps exist showing a large river flowing down along the eastern border of the county toward the La Noria mesa in Texas, and forming what is now known as 'the lost river.'" It continued that

Billy the Kid's famous tintype.

John LeMay

Josiah Gregg wrote of the Salinas Mission System and Gran Quivira in his classic work *Commerce of the Prairies* in his chapter entitled "Mines of New Mexico" on pages 116-117:

Among these ancient ruins the most remarkable are those of *La Gran Quivira*, about 100 miles southward from Santa Fe. This appears to have been a considerable city, larger and richer by far than the present capital of New Mexico has ever been. Many walls, particularly those of churches, still stand erect amid the desolation that surrounds them, as if their sacredness had been a shield against which Time dealt his blows in vain. The style of architecture is altogether superior to anything at present to be found north of Chihuahua – being of hewn stone, a building material wholly unused in New Mexico. What is more extraordinary still, is, that there is no water within less than some 10 miles of the ruins; yet we find several stone cisterns, and remains of aqueducts eight or ten miles in length, leading from the neighboring mountains, from whence water was no doubt conveyed. And, as there seem to be no indications whatever of the inhabitants' ever having been engaged in agricultural pursuits, what could have induced the rearing of a city in such an arid, woodless plain as this, except the proximity of some valuable mine, it is difficult to imagine. From the peculiar character of the place and the remains of the cisterns still existing, the object of pursuit in this case would seem to have been a *placer*, a name applied to mines of gold-dust intermixed with the earth. However, other mines have no doubt been worked in the adjacent mountains, as many spacious pits are found, such as are usually dug in pursuit of ores of silver, etc.; and it is stated that in several places heaps of scoria are still to be seen.

By some persons these ruins have been supposed to be the remains of an ancient Pueblo or aboriginal city. That is not probable, however; for though the relics of aboriginal temples might possibly be mistaken for those of Catholic churches, yet it is not to be presumed that the Spanish coat of arms would be found sculptured and painted upon their façades, as is the case in more than one instance. The most rational accounts represent this to have been a wealthy Spanish city before the general massacre of 1680, in which calamity the inhabitants perished – all except one, as the story goes; and that their immense treasures were buried in the ruins. Some credulous adventurers have lately visited the spot in search of these long-lost coffers, but as yet none have been found.

108

In 1690 a terrible volcanic earthquake disturbed all this country, the river disappeared and the malpais before mentioned were thrown up. Investigations made by the Smithsonian department reveal the fact that in the ruins of Gran Quivira Spaniards only were found in the graveyards and Pueblos in the houses. The fact is certain therefore that the evacuation of the place took place before the earthquake, and therefore about 1680, the date of the revolution. How much of this is myth and how much truth, it is impossible to tell.

The *Santa Fe New Mexican* of July 19, 1899 closely associated the Carrizozo lava beds, pictured above, with Gran Quivira. They wrote:

Between the ruins of the old town and the railroad are the great Malpais, or Gran Quivira lava beds, the most recent of the volcanic upheavals in the southwest. The crater of this now extinct volcano is located about five miles south of Gran Quivira, and is to all appearances bottomless. A large spring flows out from the south end of the Malpais, whose waters are 18 percent salt. Strange to say, myriads of a peculiar species of fish are to be found in this salt water. They are the only living creature found in it, and they seem to thrive there.

The myth of the volcanic eruption was repeated again in the *Santa Fe New Mexican* of July 19, 1899, which wrote that twenty years after the Pueblo Revolt, the Spaniards returned to find Gran Quivira in ruins, having "been destroyed by a volcanic eruption." It continued that "the Malpais had been thrown up" and "the town was found a heap of ruins." As evidence, the *New Mexican* noted, "To bear out these old traditions, Spaniards' remains are to be found in the graveyard, while Indian skeletons are found in the ruins of the houses."

In November of 1909, President Taft turned the area into Gran Quivira National Monument, and over time, the true story of Gran Quivira became known. No longer was it a "lost civilization" decimated like Atlantis before it by a volcano. By that time, experts had figured out that Little Black Peak had erupted long before Gran Quivira had been built, much less abandoned. Though the real explanation for the pueblo's abandonment was perhaps a bit less exciting than an exploding volcano, the ruins themselves are no less grand and are certainly worth a visit.

Chapter Notes

---

[1] Although some of John Meadows' reminiscences were sometimes considered suspect, for what it's worth, Billy the Kid's whereabouts between March 10 and May 1880 are wide open. Or, that is to say, there are no records of where Billy the Kid may have been at that time to contradict Meadows' account.

[2] Meadows, *Pat Garrett and Billy the Kid as I Knew Them*, pp.30-31.

12

STONE TOWERS OF GALLINAS
A History of Violence

Some of New Mexico's more enigmatic ruins comprise the stone towers of Gallinas in the northwestern portion of the state. Unlike the rounded torreons common in New Mexico, most of the Gallinas towers were rectangular and thought to have been about thirty feet tall when they stood. Constructed by crude blocks of sandstone and held in place by adobe mortar, the six-foot thick walls suggested fairly advanced masonry skills for the time. Some thought the mysterious towers may have been constructed for food storage. Others speculated the towers might have served as signal stations, capable of relaying signs from long distances from one high-top tower to another. However, ladders made of lashed poles used to climb to the top pointed to them being used as defensive structures. A second ladder then extended from the top to the bottom of the inside of the tower, which had no lower-level exterior exit. As such, the top ladder could be withdrawn to make the tower unscalable.

As perplexing as the towers themselves were the gruesome remains found therein. Clearly, the mangled corpses suggested that the victims met their ends violently. In one pit house alone in the vicinity of Rattlesnake Point, a pile of ten skeletons was found. It was thought that the ten people were thrown into the pit together for mass execution by a firing squad of arrows. Prior to their deaths, they may have been tortured, as several fingers and toes appeared to have been severed. Another tower yielded sixteen dead bodies also riddled with arrows.

Illustration of the towers that appeared in an old Canadian newspaper.

As far as we know, the towers weren't discovered by modern man until 1934, when a cowboy named Joe Arellano was gold prospecting in the Rio Gallina region. Instead of finding gold, Arellano kept stumbling across circular rock ruins clearly of prehistoric origin. Some of these were the bases of the collapsed towers, though the area sported a wide range of ruins. In addition to the collapsed tower bases, pit houses, above-ground structures, and cliff dwellings were found.

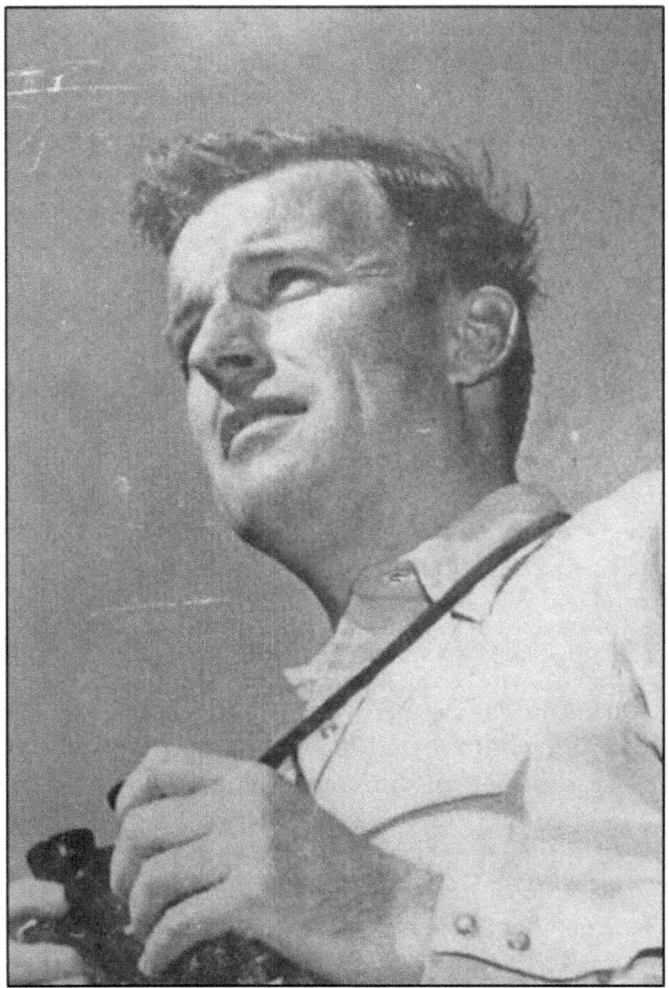

Dr. Frank C. Hibben's author photo for his book, *The Lost Americans*.

The area was thoroughly studied by University of New Mexico anthropologist Dr. Frank C. Hibben and his students in the 1950s. The most unique structure found by Hibben was thirty feet in diameter and thirty-five feet high. Dr. Hibben presumed it probably had a parapet around the top with pointed stakes. It was called the "Tower of the Two Old Men" due to the two dead bodies found therein. One had been struck with an arrow in the chest and the other in the back of the neck. Also intriguing was the fact that many of the ruins had suffered fires.

Remains of three to four bodies were found in another section of the burned ruins, and since they were not arranged in any type of burial position, it was presumed they were killed in an attack as well. As for the fires, they were thought to have been set by the survivors, both as a way of discouraging reoccupation by their enemies and also out of fear of remnants being used in witchcraft ceremonies.

Interestingly, the *Albuquerque Journal* of October 18, 1953 reported,

> Sooner or later, possibly after 100 years in some cases, most of the destroyed towers were rebuilt and lived in again. A strange feature of each of these re-entries was that a new floor of adobe and sandstone was installed over everything in the tower, including bodies or skeletons. Dr. Hibben believes some taboo may have prohibited movement of the slain tribesmen from their houses.

Just who the inhabitants were was puzzling, as they were clearly different from the Pueblo Indians. Tree ring dates from the surviving roof beams suggested the houses were built around 1003 A.D. The inhabitants only stayed in the area for a few hundred years before they were either forced to flee or left of their own free will. To this day, who the Gallinas peoples were fighting remains a mystery, but by the end of the 13th century the survivors had fled the area.

13

TERROR OF BLACK MESA

Secret of San Idelfonso

Among the pantheon on New Mexico's enchanted plateaus is Black Mesa. Simply named for the color created by the volcanic rock from which it sprang, Black Mesa lords over San Ildefonso Pueblo. Its fantastic history runs the gamut of the Pueblo Revolt, fearsome giants, and mysterious underground tunnels. The mesa was regarded by all the Puebloans of the upper Rio Grande as Tunjo, a sacred fire mountain. As evidence of this could be found ancient fire shrines on the mesa, thought to be over one thousand years old.

In 1680, the indigenous peoples of New Mexico revolted against their Spanish overlords and expelled them from the land. Having reclaimed the Kingdom of New Spain as their own, the native peoples of New Mexico ruled their lands for the next decade. However, by the early 1890s, the Spaniards were again making advances on their old territory. The reconquest was mostly bloodless as it turned out—but not in the vicinity of Black Mesa. When the people of San Ildefonso heard of the return of the Spanish, they sought refuge atop the mesa and built a few stone structures there. From atop the mesa, they held off the advances of General Diego de Vargas for months. Vargas claimed that the fortress-like mesa housed around 2,000 warriors, though historians think Vargas was likely exaggerating. Off and on from January until

September of 1894, the people atop the mesa fended off the advances of the Spaniards.[1] Vargas only triumphed when he cut off their food supplies in the land below, and finally, San Ildefonso was back under Spanish rule.[2]

Postcard depicting San Idelfonso Pueblo with Black Mesa in the background.

According to legend, an even more fantastic confrontation took place on the mesa long before the Spanish ever reconquered New Spain. Many years ago, during the days of the monster-slaying Hero Twins,[3] Black Mesa was home to the fearsome giant, Tsaviyo. Stories naturally varied, and most accounts had Tsaviyo living within a hidden cave in the mesa, while others had him perched atop Camel Rock, a nearby formation south of San Idelfonso. The giant was also said to alternate between Black Mesa and Buckman Mesa. Though located thirteen miles to the north, Tsaviyo was said to be able to walk between the two mesas in only a few steps.

Wherever he called home, the giant was a nuisance who raided the pueblos for people. Whether good or bad, he would abduct humans and return to his lair to make a meal of them. Being monster slayers, it was up to the Hero Twins to stop him. To do so, they tricked Tsaviyo into swallowing them whole. Once in his belly, they fired arrows into his heart, destroying it. In a twist, the twins decided that Tsaviyo could be put to good use, though, and so they replaced his evil heart with a new one. This new heart made Tsaviyo desire only to devour the wicked and evil. From then on, only bad people and evildoers were at risk of being eaten by the giant. Naturally, he became the de facto boogeyman that mothers spoke of to frighten their misbehaving children.[4]

Beloved New Mexico writer Alice Bullock explored Black Mesa in the 1960s with her friend, Ruth McPherson. Bullock noted that, curiously, the lava rock mesa was topped with stones from riverbeds that did not belong there. "How did they get there?" she mused in the *Santa Fe New Mexican* of October 26, 1969, then added, "There are thousands upon thousands of them." Bullock and McPherson also found what appeared to be a sacred stone. "One circle of volcanic rock centered with a white boulder was found on the side of the mesa facing the road leading to Puye. The boulder has two deep man-made indentations and two lesser ones, the sacred 'four' of the Tewa world. Could this be an earth navel of the Tewa?" she wondered. In *Forgotten Tales of New Mexico*, author Ellen Dornan noted that this white boulder was thought to be the remains of the giant's heart.[5] This isn't entirely surprising since many Native American cultures had tales of "stone giants".

An alternative tale told that Tsaviyo lived atop the mesa along with his wife and daughter, also giants. In this case, the Hero Twins managed to wrangle him in heavy chains and entomb him in a cave on the north side of the mesa. This explained strange noises emanating from within the cavern, the idea being that they were the angry bellows of the chained giant.[6] Yet another variation of the story had the Hero Twins actually killing Tsaviyo and burying him beneath the mesa somewhere. As for what the Hero Twins did with the other two giants, it is said that they tricked the daughter into a formation known as the Giant's Oven. In what was basically the Pueblo equivalent of the Hansel and Gretel story, the twins tricked the daughter into crawling into the same oven she often baked her victims in so that she was roasted to death herself.[7]

Black Mesa would not be complete without a few treasure tales. Like many areas in New Mexico, Black Mesa was thought to have been the home to a lost Spanish mine at one point. More unique was the case of a wealthy woman from Illinois who had psychic visions and dreams of a treasure within Black Mesa in 1892. She convinced four partners to go to the expense and trouble of having a deep shaft sunk into the lava rock. The tunnel went seventy-five feet into the mesa and twelve feet down. The results unfortunately bore neither treasure nor giant bones—just more lava rock.

There are also tales of labyrinthian mazes within the mesa. Like the Greek Minotaur, it was in this abode that the giant tormented his victims. Giants aside, people do believe that several tunnels extend beneath the mesa, and one supposedly goes as far as Santa Fe. Another tunnel connects to the village of Chimayo, which houses the sacred shrine of blessed earth. Sacred fires were sometimes lit in a cave outside of Chimayo, and smoke from these fires would waft through the underground tunnels until they seeped out of Black Mesa, fifteen miles away. Or, at least, that's what some people claim.

Ultimately, whether it houses the bones of giants and a secret tunnel system or not, Black Mesa certainly has a rich history.

Chapter Notes

---

[1] A legend associated with the siege told of the women cutting off their long hair to make a rope with. This rope was then used to haul supplies up the mesa.

[2] The people of San Idelfonso would successfully revolt again in 1696, destroying the local mission before the pueblo was again recaptured by the Spanish.

[3] One variation named the twins Youth and Fireboy.

[4] Tsaviyo, it seems, was later conjoined with the Spanish folktale of El Abuelo, a boogeyman who showed up to whip unruly children, especially at Christmas.

[5] Dornan, *Forgotten Tales of New Mexico*, pp.145-146.

[6] Considering some reports say that the noises of rattling chains and shrieks were heard only on the Good Friday Eve, it's possible that a band of penitentes were using a cave within the mesa where they committed self-flagellation.

[7] What happened to the wife of the giant remains untold, so far as this author can tell.

SAN IDELFONSO'S GOLDEN PYRAMID

A PYRAMID OF GOLD.

A Pueblo Indian of San Idelfonso, a little town on the Rio Grande; some twenty-three miles west of Santa Fe, is the only living possessor of an equally valuable secret. A great many years ago some Indians of that pueblo were hunting in the mountains, to the west of the river, when they discovered a point of yellowy metal projecting from the earth. Dismounting from their horses they began to dig; and soon found that they had to do with a pyramid of pure gold, of apparently endless depth. With their axes they chopped off all their animals could carry, and covered the deposit so that others might not find it. A few days later they left for Mexico, where they traded their gold for horses and such other personal property as is dear to an Indian's heart. After their return to New Mexico they visited the golden pyramid frequently, and hacked off the wherewithal to buy whatever they desired and to make presents to their friends. At last all had gone over to the happy hunting grounds save one, and he was well along in years. Once he was captured by Mexicans, who had frequently seen him with chunks of gold, and was clapped into a prison to make him tell whence he got *tanto oro*.

He steadfastly refused to tell, despite the ingenious 'persuasions' of his captors, and his obstinacy was about to be rewarded with death. Finally, acting on the advice of relatives, he got friends to club together the gold that he had given them, and with it to "salt" a certain spot which he designated. Then he told the Mexicans he would lead them to his gold-bed if they would let him go, and did conduct them to the salted spot. They found several thousand dollars' worth or gold there, and were so delighted that they set him free. When this old man was on his deathbed he called in three of his most intimate friends and told them exactly where the Gold Pyramid really was, charging them to work it for the maintenance of his family. Two of them died soon after: but the third still lives in San Ildefonso. He has never told but one white man of his momentous secret, and I doubt if he has told any one else. Last winter he came to this white man and detailed the circumstances, saying, "You are the best friend we have ever had. I will take you to this place and show you the gold, for I know you will treat me fairly about it. It is in such and such a canyon, in the fourth arroyo, up-stream from a certain rock. As soon as the snow is gone I will come for you, and we will go up there together." He failed to come as agreed, and when seen later, said that he did not dare go yet, as some of the Indians suspected his secret, and were watching every move he made. — *St. Louis Globe-Democrat* (February 17, 1889)

14

PECOS PUEBLO
Kingdom of Montezuma

O f all the deserted pueblo remains in New Mexico, those at Pecos are some of the largest. Pecos Pueblo also hosted more legends than nearly any other pueblo in the state. When Coronado came across it on his march towards the Seven Cities of Gold, it was called Cicuye by the Spaniards. There, he and his men met a trickster called "the Turk," who ingeniously led the Spaniards all the way to Salinas, Kansas, in search of the Seven Cities of Gold. Thus, Cicuye managed to peacefully get rid of the Spaniards... for a time at least.

Pecos Pueblo was established around 1350 A.D. and boasted a population of about 2,000 residents, making it one of the largest pueblos in the region. However, by the mid-1800s, the population had dwindled to such an extent that the pueblo had to be abandoned completely. The main cause of loss was disease introduced by the Spaniards, aided along by Comanche raids. In August of 1838, twenty-one survivors of the once great pueblo migrated to Jemez Pueblo, where they were welcomed due to both pueblos sharing a common lineage.

Having been deserted shortly before the Mexican-American War, the ruins of Pecos Pueblo were especially enigmatic for Anglo settlers and explorers. For instance, the main ruin was called the "Astek Church" by artist John Mix Stanley in 1846, when he sketched the pueblo. Shortly after, another legend of the church was recorded by a private in the army, Josiah M. Rice, who passed through Pecos in 1851 with Colonel Edwin V. Sumner. Rice recorded,

> There are many traditions connected with this old church, one of which is that it was built by a race of giants, fifty feet in height. But these, dying off, they were succeeded by dwarfs, with red heads who, being in their turn exterminated, were followed by the Aztecs.

John Mix Stanley's rendition of Pecos Pueblo.

Along the same lines, the *Connersville Examiner* of October 10, 1883, printed a letter out of Las Vegas that stated, "Near by [the church] are some boulders having in them distinct imprints of human feet, as plain as if they were in soft clay, and the tradition is that these are prints of Montezuma's feet when he left."[1]

The paper spoke not of the historical Montezuma, who ruled Mexico during the conquest, but of a mythical version. Better known among the indigenous peoples as Poheyemo, this god-man became intermingled with Montezuma over the ages. Poheyemo was said to be born of a virgin in the nearby pueblo of Pose Uingge (now a large prehistoric ruin). Poheyemo was an odd child who preferred to converse with animals and invisible spirits rather than other children. As a young man, when the tribal medicine man died, lots were drawn to choose his successor. Poheyemo was chosen through this process, much to the chagrin of older men. However, Poheyemo soon demonstrated special powers such as the ability to locate abundant game and call down rain from the heavens to water the crops. In no time, he was revered by all. However, the elders at his pueblo eventually angered him and so he traveled south to Pecos Pueblo. There he chose the new name of Montezuma for himself, and the once small pueblo grew into one of the largest settlements in the region.

Pecos Pueblo as photographed by the author. To native speakers, it was P`ae'kilâ, meaning "the place above the water."

Montezuma ruled over Pecos until the Great Spirit sent a giant eagle to take him away. Montezuma flew southward, with new pueblos springing in his wake until finally he arrived at the spot of Tenochtitlán in Mexico. However, before he departed, Montezuma instructed his disciples to light a sacred flame upon the altar of the sun, and to keep it burning at all times. If they did so, one day he would return.

"The Watch for Montezuma" by Jules Tavernier.

It should be noted that the Spaniards didn't arrive until long after the mythical version of Montezuma traveled to Mexico. But, after their coming, the legend was tweaked so that Montezuma might return one day to expel the Spanish invaders. This begat a tradition observed by many early-day explorers wherein the peoples of the pueblos would watch for Montezuma's return every morning as the sun rose.

In addition to the sacred flame, Montezuma also left a darker legacy behind in the form of a gigantic snake, sometimes known as Montezuma's serpent. For many years, tales persisted that the people of Pecos Pueblo kept a giant snake in a cave with a sacred fire, presumably linked to the eternal flame said to grant immortality. This giant rattlesnake was so big that human beings were occasionally given to it as a sacrifice. As opposed to the extinguishing of the sacred flame, either the death or the departure of the great serpent was yet another reason used to explain the abandonment of Pecos Pueblo.

Believe it or not, Montezuma's flame itself was not purely folkloric. Many pioneers of the day attested to having seen it. Among the better-known ones was Josiah Gregg, who recorded seeing the flame in *Commerce of the Prairies*:

I have myself descended into the famous *estufas*, or subterranean vaults, of which there were several in the village, and have beheld this consecrated fire, silently smouldering under a covering of ashes, in the basin of a small altar. Some say that they never lost hope in the final coming of Montezuma until, by some accident or other, or a lack of a sufficiency of warriors to watch it, the fire became extinguished; and that it was this catastrophe that induced them to abandon their villages, as I have before observed.[2]

Though disease and Comanche raids are the historically accepted reason for Pecos Pueblo's abandonment, as Gregg alluded to, many others blamed it on the flame being extinguished. In one version of the legend, Montezuma entrusted twelve virgin daughters of the pueblo leaders to keep the flame lit. However, one night, one of the girls let the flame extinguish, thus explaining why Montezuma never returned and why the pueblo had to be abandoned.

Postcard of Pecos Pueblo ruins.

A later letter, dated October 4, 1883, out of nearby Las Vegas also recorded a variation of the desertion of Pecos Pueblo and presented yet another fate for the eternal flame:

In 1837 the tribe was reduced to 15 persons, of whom but seven were warriors. All this time they had kept the sacred fire burning, but they could do it no longer, as they were too few, and tradition says that three warriors went into the woods with the fire and that Montezuma himself appeared and relieved them of it. Then they packed their goods and went to join their brothers at the Jemez Pueblo, west of the Rio Grande.[3]

Yet one more account of the Sacred Flame's ultimate fate came from roving journalist Matthew C. Field. In 1839, Field spent the night in the old Pecos Church and wrote an article on the legend of the pueblo. According to him, in its last days, the peoples of Pecos had chopped down so many trees to keep the sacred fire burning that the land was becoming barren. He claimed that eventually, only the chief, his daughter, and her betrothed remained. The old man died, and so the daughter and her mate went to the hidden cave and retrieved the sacred fire via a brand, which they carried with them into the wilderness. The night sky then lit up with a red glow and "the lovers lay in each other's arms, kissing death from each other's lips, and smiling to see the fire of Montezuma mounting up to heaven."[4] Considering that Field was also an actor with a flare for the dramatic, it's likely he simply made this version of the legend up.

These are but a few of many alternate fates for the sacred flame being extinguished. Though the flame itself may be long gone, it will always keep the legend of Pecos Pueblo burning bright.

Chapter Notes

[1] Mexico has similar legends at spots where Quetzalcoatl left his footprints, and so on.

[2] Gregg, *Commerce of the Prairies*, pp.57-58.

[3] "FROM NEW MEXICO," *The Clermont Sun* (October 9, 1883), p.4.

[4] Porter and Sunder, *Matt Field on the Santa Fe Trail*, p.250.

Pueblo Bonito, early 1900s.

15

CHACO CANYON
Grand Complex of the Anasazi

L ocated in northwestern New Mexico between Farmington and Albuquerque, Chaco Canyon is the crown jewel of New Mexico's many ancient ruins. Not only is it considered unique in New Mexico, but its structures are considered to be some of the most important pre-Columbian ruins in all of North and Central America. Adding to their allure is the fact that, to this day, it's unknown what happened to the inhabitants of the magnificent ancient cities that made up the Chaco Canyon complex.

What is known is that it was inhabited by the Anasazi between 900 A.D. and 1150 A.D. At its height, it is estimated that 5,000 people or more lived in the 75 settlements in the canyon. Among the largest and most significant were Chetro Ketl, Una Vida, Pueblo Alto, Peñasco Blanco, and Pueblo Bonito, which stretched across two acres and was once four stories high. Comprised of sandstone blocks and timber hauled from great distances, they were the largest buildings in North America until the 19th century.

Also of great significance was the area's road system. Satellite imaging has confirmed that there are eight main roads, thirty feet wide and running more than 180 miles. They were created by paving a smooth, leveled surface into the bedrock by removing vegetation and soil. Occasionally, they are flanked by crude walls and berms.

Pueblo Bonito, Chaco Canyon National Monument

The term Anasazi was coined in 1927 via the archaeological Pecos Classification system, and referred to the people of the Ancestral Pueblos in what is today the Four Corners region. To the Navajo, Anasazi meant "ancient enemy." Among the other fantastic ruins they left were Arizona's Cliff Palace and Montezuma Castle. Though not tucked away in a cliff, the ruins of Chaco Canyon are sprawling by comparison.

The roads lead from Pueblo Bonito, Chetro Ketl, and Una Vida towards smaller, outlier sites in addition to significant natural features nearby, like lakes and streams. Archeologists and anthropologists alike puzzle over whether the road system was primarily for economic purposes or religious ones. Odds favored the roads being used in the trading system, utilized to transport goods to and from Chaco Canyon. That Chaco Canyon was a trading hub is indisputable considering that seashells and macaws, obviously from Mexico, were present there. Analysis of strontium isotopes in the wooden beams showed that much of the timber was transported there from distant mountain ranges.

As stated before, it's unconfirmed why the Anasazi vacated the once-great cities. War with another race or drought comprise the more grounded theories, while others think the Anasazi may have entered another dimension altogether. Wherever they disappeared to, many of their possessions were mysteriously left behind, and some of the dwellings were burned. The possessions being left behind is especially curious due to fear of witchcraft. If a witch or an enemy gained a former belonging, they could be used to inflict witchcraft. As such, said possessions should have been destroyed entirely or taken with the residents when they relocated.

Pueblo Del Arroyo Kiva at Chaco Canyon. (Historic American Buildings Survey).

There is also chilling evidence for cannibalism in Chaco Canyon in the form of dismembered bodies found at two sites within the central canyon. The Navajo considered Chaco Canyon to be a place of evil and witchcraft at one time, where corpse powder was created. Along those lines, some have thought the dead remains found in Chaco Canyon were those of witches. This wouldn't explain the dead bodies of the children, though, who were too young to have been considered witches. The Navajo believed that the evil magic enacted in Chaco Canyon resulted in the world bringing about a great fire and earthquake to extinguish them.

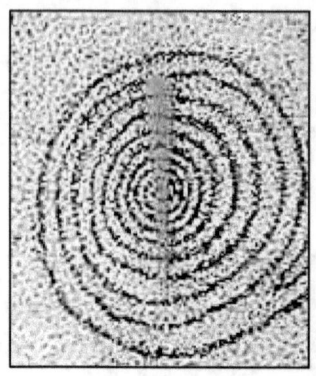

Diagram showing the location of the sun daggers on the summer solstice. (National Park Service)

Talks of cannibalism are tame in comparison to other theories about Chaco Canyon's desertion. In fact, what we could consider conspiracy theories on Chaco Canyon have run wild for years. Some have even drawn parallels to structures photo-graphed on Mars by NASA's Voyager program in the summer of 1976 and Chaco Canyon. While Chaco Canyon's ties to Mars are certainly open to interpretation, indisputable evidence can be found tying the complex to astronomy.

The most notable petroglyph at Chaco is easily the "Sun Dagger" at Fajada Butte. It was discovered in 1977 by an artist named Anna Sofaer, working as a volunteer cataloging the rock art. One day, she discovered three large stone slabs that leaned against the cliff, which channeled sunlight and shadow markings onto two spiral petroglyphs on the cliff wall. On her next visit, she discovered what she initially called a "dagger of light" bisecting one of the spirals. Upon further study, it was learned that the Sun Dagger actually denoted the solstices and the equinoxes, indicating that the Chacoans had an advanced grasp of astronomy. Upon figuring this out, experts took another look at the many buildings at the complex and figured out that they, too, were aligned with solar and lunar cycles alike.

Does this association with the stars imply some kind of otherworldly exit for the Anasazi? Not necessarily, but it's certainly interesting to ponder.

16

ROSWELL'S LOST RIVER
Southeastern New Mexico's Underground Secret

North of Roswell is a desolate stretch of desert land that writer Georgia B. Redfield once described as a place of "downright, flesh creeping spookiness, especially on a dismal rainy late evening..." Redfield, who was a correspondent for the *Times* in the 1930s and 1940s, spoke not of the notorious UFO crash site, also located north of Roswell, but of Lost River. The Lost River was located nine miles northeast of Roswell and about five miles north of the old Clovis Highway. The place was so named because most of the river actually flowed underground, linking through a series of caves and grottoes.

Today, the Lost River is truly lost, as it no longer exists. Redfield recorded her memory of it in the 1930s, describing the "dangerous looking, caving, dead river banks" which cut "a zigzag course east through the most weird, deserted section of country in southeastern New Mexico."

One of the more interesting stories to spring from the area concerned an old Hispanic sheepherder. The man was digging a well in the area of Lost River when he fell into an underground lake. Redfield wrote,

> After his morning's work...he climbed out of the ten foot opening he had made, ate his lunch, then jumped back into the well to resume his digging, and dropped

twenty feet into a lake below. He was almost paralyzed from fright, but seeing light in the distance he began swimming and wading through shallow water until he reached safety on the banks of Lost River, half a mile below the pool, or lake, into which he had dropped.[1]

Lost River. (Historical Society for Southeast New Mexico)

Other stories said that an old horse trough along with a coat was found in one of the Lost River caves in 1893. In the coat's pocket was said to be the bill of sale for several thousand head of cattle from a "former, long departed, cattleman." Could it have been John Chisum's? Another tale said the cave was used by a counterfeiter's ring long ago. There, in the darkness, they made their counterfeit dollars. Though this is unlikely, there was a real counterfeit ring in nearby White Oaks in 1879, of which Billy the Kid was naturally said to be a part.

Outlaws hangout or not, Lost River was a dangerous spot. In 1924, a man and woman had parked their automobile on a riverbank and then walked down below to look at the river. The car collapsed the bank above them, crushing the couple. After that, the cave and its crumbling banks were dynamited to prevent further tragedies. However, another tragedy would still befall the location.

About ten years later, on May 22, 1935, two couples from Illinois, Mr. and Mrs. George Lorius and Mr. and Mrs. Albert Herberer, disappeared while traveling through New Mexico in their automobile. Apparently, they were last seen in Vaughn before they seemingly dropped off the face of the earth.

An anonymous tip claimed the couple's car crashed into a lake north of Roswell in the vicinity of Lost River, and so the lake was dragged in search of the bodies and the vehicle. When nothing turned up, a deep-sea diver out of Houston, TX, came along and scoured the lake bottom, looking in every crevice. Though no bodies were found, one interesting discovery was made: "A missing touring car, however, on which insurance had been collected, was found (with tires still inflated) and was raised to the surface."[2] Stranger yet, it was later learned this car did not belong to Mr. Lorius, for his car was found sometime later in Dallas.

Lost River. (Historical Society for Southeast New Mexico)

On June 29, 1935, two Albuquerque cowboys out riding their cattle range actually came across the couple's burned luggage and alerted the authorities. This led to the police following a trail of forged travelers checks belonging to Mr. Lorius all the way into Texas, hence the car being discovered in Dallas. As to the alleged murderer, there had been a man with a tattoo on one arm last seen driving the car, but he was never caught.

Lost River. (Historical Society for Southeast New Mexico)

So, was the search at Lost River just a wild goose chase? Perhaps not. Later, a second tip, this time from an unidentified man from a penitentiary, said that the couples' bodies could be found northeast of Roswell in the vicinity of Lost River. Since the bodies were never found anywhere else, perhaps they could have been swept away in Roswell's Lost River?

Today, what was once Lost River is well known in the Southwest as Bitter Lakes National Wildlife Refuge and has long since left its past as a place of mystery and tragedy behind.

Chapter Notes

[1] Redfield, "Yesterday and Today," n.d.
[2] Ibid.

17

SHRINE OF THE STONE LIONS
Bandelier Monument Mystery

L ocated within the southern boundaries of Bandelier National Monument are two of the most unique stone carvings in the Southwest. About ten miles from the monument's headquarters, outside of Frijoles Canyon, is Pajarito Plateau. Along one of the high, narrow mesas called Potrero de las Vacas lie two sleeping stone lions. The Shrine of the Stone Lions, as it is formally known, is encircled by rocks. As for the stone effigies, they are life-sized at six-feet long and two-feet high, though admittedly, erosion and the elements have made them nearly unrecognizable today. In fact, some might mistake them for giant lizards due to their tails.

They were carved into the soft bedrock of two side-by-side boulders near Yapashe, an ancient pueblo ruin. However, if they were carved by the former occupants is unknown. Furthermore, when exactly they were carved is uncertain as well, but one thing is certain; they are very, very old. Nor are these the only two. Several miles to the south, outside of the monument's boundaries, can be found another stone lion. Actually, there used to be two. This second pair occupied the Potrero de los Idolos mesa. Unfortunately, one of them was destroyed about seventy years or so ago with dynamite by a treasure hunter who thought that, perhaps, the stone lion capped a treasure hole. The other lion survived and is reportedly still recognizable, though.

Some have theorized that of the two figures comprising the Shrine of the Stone Lions, one is a lion and the other is actually a jaguar. If the case of the latter is true, this could link the "stone lions" to the religions of Mesoamerica. The Aztecs, in particular, had some interesting beliefs regarding jaguars. Namely, in the creation story, it was said that monstrous jaguars were utilized by the gods to destroy the creations of the first world. (National Parks Service Photo)

The two stone lions within Bandelier National Monument are revered by several different pueblos to this day. The residents of Cochiti Pueblo, ten miles to the south, venerate the effigies by placing offerings to them. It is thought that members of a secret hunting society of the Cochiti are the ones leaving behind the offerings. To them, it is the sacred place of Mokatc, a panther god of the Cochiti. It is thought that, perhaps, the ancestors of the Cochiti who lived at Yapashi made the carvings, though this is unverified. Contrary to this, in the 1880s, the Cochiti told Adolph Bandelier that they were carved by the peoples of Kuapa, a ruin near Cochiti, which coexisted with the Yapashi.

Interestingly, the residents of Zuni Pueblo, 200 miles away, also venerate the stone lions, making long pilgrimages to the shrine. The Zunis believe that the stone lions were the guardians of the place of emergence, called Shipapolima. Like many other tribes, the Zuni believed that they emerged from the underworld to the surface. (The place was also the home of the first man, called Poshaiyanki.) The fact that both the Zuni and the Cochiti venerate the lions would seem to imply that the effigies predate both tribes.

There is also another shrine sporting a single stone lion as well. It, too, is outside of Bandelier National Monument. For its protection, the exact location is kept a secret, but like the others, it sits atop a lonely mesa. Like its brethren, it is encompassed by a ring of rocks as well.

Jack Kutz wrote of what appeared to be paranormal activity associated with that statue in his book *Mysteries & Miracles of New Mexico*. Kutz related how a team of anthropologists from the University of New Mexico worked tirelessly to transport the stone lion to a museum to protect it from vandals on March 7, 1970. However, the operation was plagued with a string of bad luck eerily preceded by an eclipse of the sun that day. In addition to an injury that ensued from a falling boulder when moving the statue, a helicopter used to transport the stone lion also experienced difficulties from harsh winds, and the stone lion nearly crushed one of the anthropologists as it was being lowered onto a truck bed below. The stone lion was taken to the Maxwell Museum, but eventually the lion was returned due to protests by the people of San Felipe Pueblo in 1981. Unfortunately, the lion now lacks its tail.

Along those same supernatural lines, the stone lions also played a small part in a witchcraft scare at the pueblo of Abiquiú in the 1760s. For a time, it was thought that the sorcerers of Abiquiú derived their power from pagan monuments outside of the pueblo. Two of these pagan effigies included what sounded to be some stone lions. They were said to have been located either within or very close to the current-day Bandelier National Monument south of Abiquiú. These stone lions were destroyed by the main priest at Abiquiú, Father Toledo. Later, a woman who was allegedly possessed told Father Toledo that in destroying the effigies, he had lessened the powers of the evil ones.

Supernatural or not, it can only be hoped that the stone lions survive into the next century to puzzle a new generation.

18

THE SEVEN CITIES OF GOLD
The Kingdom of Cibola

Within the current-day confines of the Zuni Indian Reservation in western New Mexico lies the remains of a once great pueblo. Called Háwikuh, it was built by the Zuni sometime between 1200-1400 A.D. and occupied by them up until the Great Pueblo Revolt of 1680. Today, the site is a National Historic Landmark District accessible via the Zuni Pueblo Department of Tourism.[1] With the aid of a guide, a hiking trail will take one to ruins of sandstone and adobe that are somewhat inauspicious if one doesn't know their history. As it was, these simple ruins were once thought to hold the wealth of what the Spaniards called the "New World."

As one of several pueblo villages within the Zuni nation, Háwikuh was thought to be Cibola, the first of the mythical Seven Cities of Gold. Though Cibola has gone down in history as the best-remembered of the seven, it was only the first of the seven. Among the known names of its sister cities were Marata, Ahacus, and Totonteac, the largest of them all. The seven cities were not, contrary to some misconceptions, thought to have been constructed of pure gold. Nor did the myth of the seven cities originate in the Americas.

In actuality, the legend of the Seven Cities of Gold existed seven hundred years before Columbus sailed the ocean blue. So the story went; when the Moors invaded the Iberian

Peninsula in the 8th century, seven Portuguese bishops set sail across the Atlantic. On their ships were stored treasure hordes of unimaginable wealth. It was believed that these seven bishops settled somewhere in the New World, where they founded seven enchanted cities of great wealth. And indeed, when the Spanish conquistadors arrived on the shores of Mexico, they were at once told of a land of great riches to the north.[2] As such, it was thought these must have been the cities founded by the seven bishops.

Ruins of Háwikuh c.1886.

"What was it about the seven bishops who had fled Portugal centuries ago?" Paul Horgan wrote in *Conquistadors in North American History*. He elaborated,

> Everyone had heard how they must have founded seven cities in the New World. Somewhere in the northern lands, now, Indians declared that there were seven rich cities, together called Cibola, and everyone ... wondered if these could be the cities of the persecuted bishops."[3]

The first inklings of the Seven Cities of Gold were usually attributed to the Spanish explorer Álvar Núñez Cabeza de Vaca. Cabeza de Vaca's story began in 1528, when he was part of an expedition of 600 men, women, and slaves led by

Pánfilo de Narváez. The purpose of the voyage was to colonize Florida, which had been claimed by Ponce de León, who had tried and failed to find the Fountain of Youth there. However, Narváez's fleet was shipwrecked off the coast of Florida, and in the end, the only survivors would be four castaways in the form of Cabeza de Vaca, Alonso del Castillo Maldonado, Andrés Dorantes de Carranza, and his Moorish slave, Esteban de Dorantes.

Sometimes conflated with the seven cities of gold were the seven golden caves of the Aztec, located at a place called Aztlán. The Aztecs claimed Aztlán was far in the north, and it was from there that they emerged from the underworld to the surface. Therefore, when the Spaniards asked the indigenous peoples about seven golden cities to the north, sometimes this was confused with the legend of the seven caves of Aztlán.

The four men wandered westward from Florida for eight years. At times, they were prisoners of various Indian tribes, while at others, they were revered as faith healers. This is because once, when their captors insisted they heal the sick, the men prayed to God, and miraculously the sick were healed. Afterward, the four men were called the "Children of the Sun" and regarded as medicine men from a faraway land.

Cabeza De Vaca and his companions wandering the coastline.

In 1536, the four men finally arrived in Mexico City and told of their adventures in the interior of the unexplored New World. Contrary to popular belief, Cabeza de Vaca said nothing of Seven Cities of Gold, though he did speak of rumors of towns of great wealth. Likewise, Nuno de Guzman, the Governor of New Spain in Mexico, had heard his servant, Tejo, make similar claims years before. A Spanish chronicler of the time, Pedro de Castaneda, wrote,

> In the year 1530, Nuno de Guzman, who was president of New Spain, had in his possession an Indian, one of the natives of the Valley of Otixipar, who was called Tejo by the Spaniards. This Indian said he was the son

of a trader who was dead, but that when he was a little boy, his father had gone into the backcountry with fine feathers to trade for ornaments and that when he came back, he brought a large amount of gold and silver, of which there is a good deal in that country. He went with him once or twice and saw some very large villages, which he compared to Mexico and its environs. He had seen seven very large towns which had their streets of silver workers.

Depiction of Esteban de Dorantes.

Though de Vaca had only spoken of large pueblos to the north but no gold, Guzman assumed that perhaps de Vaca was hiding the truth and that, possibly, de Vaca wanted to mount a return expedition to secure the riches for himself. Soon after, Guzman orchestrated his own expedition of 400 men, though it was met with failure and they had to turn back due to various obstacles.

The subsequent governor of New Spain, Don Antonio de Mendoza, organized an expedition to be led by Fray Marcos de Niza. As Cabeza de Vaca had sailed back to Spain, Fray Marcos enlisted Esteban, the slave, to lead him to the seven cities. Esteban was probably the better choice over de Vaca anyway. As it was, the indigenous peoples were fascinated by Esteban's dark skin, never having seen an African before. The women, especially, were said to be taken with Esteban. In a sense, he was a "rockstar" for his day, often showered with gifts and surrounded by what could be called "groupies" for lack of a better word.

Zuni Pueblo, aka Cibola, with Mount Taylor in the background, as depicted by the Dutch painter Jan Mostaert.

Fray Marcos, Esteban, and their envoy left Culiacan on March 7, 1539, and after reaching central Sonora, Fray Marcos sent Esteban northwards "with instructions to proceed 50 or 60 leagues and see if he could find anything which might help them in their search." They had a system in place wherein Esteban would send back crosses of various sizes via his native companions. A white cross as wide as a hand with spread fingers signified something of moderate importance. For something a little more interesting, a cross two spans wide would be used. And, as an indication of wealth greater than or equal to the riches of Mexico, Esteban was to send a very large cross. Esteban had been gone only four days when Fray Marcos received a huge cross that was the height of a man. Esteban's messenger told Fray Marcos that thirty days away was "the greatest thing in the world." The message continued that there were,

Seven very great cities, all under one lord; that the houses, of stone and lime, were large, the smallest being of one story with a terrace above, and others of two and three stories, and that of the Lord had four, all joined under his rule, and in the porches of the main houses were worked many designs of turquoises, of which, he said, there was a great abundance, and that the people of those cities went very well clothed. Many other particulars he told me of these seven cities, as well as of other provinces farther away, each of which, he said, was much greater than the seven cities; and in order to comprehend it as he knew it, I asked him many questions, and I found him to be of very good intelligence.[4]

On April 8, Fray Marcos left for the village from which Esteban had sent the messenger. Upon arrival, he found Esteban had gone on ahead, but a new messenger gave Fray Marcos another cross equal to the size of the first. He urged that Fray Marcos should hurry along onto Cibola. Before doing so, the villagers described the riches ahead. They spoke little of gold and instead talked of trading labor for turquoises and finely tanned cowhides. The people there, they claimed, wore fine clothes of cotton not dissimilar to the robe Fray Marcos was wearing. As evidence of these remarks, Fray Marcos noted that the natives "gave me some cow hides so well-tanned and dressed that they appeared to be the work of men of much culture, and they said that all these had come from Cibola." Fray Marcos also said that the natives he spoke with wore "fine and beautiful turquoises" that hung "from their ears and from their noses." The natives also said that turquoises was "worked into the principal doorways of Cibola."

Fray Marcos went on his way, and the following day arrived at the next village where he found another cross from Esteban and more tales of the seven cities, in this case that of Totonteac. Looking at Fray Marcos's robe, the villagers told him that "there was a great deal of that material in Totonteac, and that the natives in that place were clothed with it." Fray

Marcos displayed some skepticism at the remarks, and the natives went on to describe the animal from which the peoples of Totonteac clothed themselves with. They claimed that "in Totonteac they have some small animals from which they take the fiber with which they make cloth like yours." Fray Marcos was surprised by the remark, never having heard of such an animal before. He continued,

> I desired to inform myself very particularly of it, and they told me that the animals are of the size of the two Castilian greyhounds that Esteban had with him: they said they had many of them in Totonteac – but I could not learn what genus of animals they were.[5]

In the same village came a particularly interesting account from a man who claimed to have escaped from Cibola. Fray Marcos wrote, "Here I found a man, a native of Cibola, who told me he had fled from the person whom the Lord had placed there in Cibola, for the Lord of these seven cities lives and has his home in one of them that they call Ahacus…" Fray Marcos explained that, according to the escaped prisoner, the kingdom of the seven cities had a ruler in each placed by the main chief. Furthermore, the man claimed that Cibola was a large city with many people crowding its streets and plazas. He said that Cibola housed towering structures ten stories high in which, on certain days of the year, all the chiefs assembled. Like earlier reports, he said the houses were made of stone and lime "and that the porches in front of the principal houses are of turquoises."

Cibola was only the start though. All of the cities to follow Cibola were even larger. Whereas others had called Totonteac the most important, this man claimed that it was "the biggest in the world and with the most people and riches." He continued that the residents dressed similarly to Fray Marcos, and again mentioned the strange, unidentified animal from which their fabric was made. Lastly, he said the people of Totonteac "had much culture and were different from those that I thus far have seen."

On his journey, Fray Marcos received proof of what he first thought to be a species of unicorn. The Indians had brought to him a hide about half as large as that of a large cow and said that it came from a creature possessing only one horn "in the front, and that this horn is curved toward its breast, and then turns in a straight point." Fray Marcos continued that they claimed that the animal "was strong enough to tear apart anything in its path and that there were thousands of them in the country to the north. Their hide looks like buckskin and the hair on it was 'as long as a finger is thick.'" At another village, Fray Marcos received another hide from what he thought might be a unicorn:

> Here in this valley they brought me a hide, half as large again as that of a large cow, and they told me it was from an animal which has only one horn on the forehead, and that this horn is curved toward the chest, and that from there it turns out in a straight point which, they say, has so much strength that nothing, no matter how hard, would fail to break if struck by it. They said that there were many of these animals in that other country: the color of the hide is like that of a goat in the hair is as long as the finger."[6]

It is thought that this hide belonged to a buffalo, though buffaloes have more than one horn, of course. Is it possible that Fray Marcos simply misunderstood the amount of horns? Or was this a heretofore unknown one-horned animal of some kind? If it was a buffalo, or the "humpbacked bull" as the Spaniards called it, then this animal was what Cibola derived its namesake from, as *cibola* meant humpbacked bull.

The "prisoner of Cibola" mentioned another independent kingdom called Ácus, where the residents slept in "beds high above the floor, with bed clothing and with canopies over the beds." Most historians concur that he was speaking of Acoma Pueblo, pictured above.

Curiously, the man noted that

> ...to the southeast is a kingdom that they call Marata, which used to have very many large settlements; that all have these houses of stone and stories, and that those towns were and still are at war with the Lord of the

seven cities, through which war this kingdom of Marata is greatly reduced in numbers, but still is on top and continues the war with the others.[7]

It was around May 9th that Fray Marcos's golden voyage came to its conclusion. An exasperated member of Esteban's envoy arrived with the news that Esteban was most likely dead. The man couldn't say for sure because the last he saw of him was as they ran for their lives from Cibola with the natives in hot pursuit. Presumably, Esteban had been struck down by an arrow and died.[8] Apparently, Esteban had sent his envoys to the mysterious leader of Cibola as he usually did. However, whereas he was usually warmly received, the "chief of Cibola" seemed incensed by Esteban's usual theatrics. Instead of a warm welcome, he forbade him and his entourage from entering the city and confined them to a house outside of the city limits. The next day, they were chased out of the city, and the survivors now stood before Fray Marcos.

Fray Marcos was no doubt discouraged to be so close to the object of his search only to be turned back. The friar told his subjects that when the Emperor learned what had happened, he would send Christian troops to Cibola to subjugate them. Fray Marcos wanted to march to Cibola and deliver this threat to their great chief, but the Indians would have none of it, claiming "that none can withstand the might of Cibola."[9]

Fray Marcos had to see the mythical city for himself, though, and marched on with a few companions to get a glimpse of it. Folklore now states that from a distance, Fray Marcos spotted a city basking in the sunset rays and mistook adobe walls for those of gold. However, if you read the account to follow, you will see that he said no such thing. Fray Marcos's testimony of Cibola is as follows:

I pursued my journey until within sight of Cibola, which is situated on a plane at the skirt of a round hill. It has the appearance of a very beautiful town, the best that I have seen in these parts. The houses are of the fashion that the Indians had described to me, all of stone, with their stories and terraces, as it appeared to me from the hill where I was able to view it. The city is bigger than the city of Mexico. At times I was tempted to go to it, because I knew that I ventured only life, which had offered to God the day I commenced the journey. At the end I feared to do so, considering my danger and that, if I died, I would not be able to make a report of this country, which to me appears the greatest and best of the discoveries.[10]

Zuni man standing before "Zuni stone idols," c. 1900.

As was custom, Fray Marcos then placed a small cross within a heap of stones and spoke forth a proclamation claiming Cibola as a territory of New Spain. Fray Marcos gave his exaggerated report in Mexico, and to this day it's debated if Fray Marcos was telling the truth as he saw it or if he deliberately exaggerated reports of what he had seen. In the ensuing conquest, under the command of Governor Francisco Vasquez de Coronado in the spring of 1540, nothing quite so grand as Cibola was found. Instead, Coronado came upon what is now considered to be Háwikuh. The Zunis put up a fight against the Spaniards, emaciated after their long journey. Despite their weakened condition, the conquistadors did what they set out to do and claimed Cibola as their own. Not only was it devoid of gold, but even the promised turquoise-adorned homes. Fray Marcos was spurned by all of the party, and had he not been a man of the cloth it's thought he would have been executed on the spot. Likewise, Totonteac was really just a pueblo along the Rio Grande, equally poor, and devoid of the great ruler that was promised. The seven cities weren't even related, and most spoke different languages.

The Coronado Expedition passing through New Mexico on the way to the Great Plains by Frederic Remington.

Where then did the accounts of both the natives and Fray Marcos stem? Did Fray Marcos fabricate the testimony of the natives in his report? Likewise, did the natives promise riches to the north simply to get rid of Fray Marcos and his party? More confusing is Fray Marcos's eyewitness claims of the great city itself. If he wasn't lying outright, could it be that Fray Marcos saw a mirage city not unlike the White Pueblo of the Malpais?

Only one thing is for certain; centuries later, Cibola has left more questions than answers in its mystical wake...

Chapter Notes

---

[1] The Zuni Nation rejected the idea of it becoming a national park.

[2] The Seven Bishops were also thought to have settled on the mythical island of Antilla, closer to Spain and sometimes called the Isle of Seven Cities.

[3] Horgan, *Conquistadors*, p.128.

[4] Hallenbeck, *Journey of Fray Marcos*, p.19.

[5] Ibid, pp.23-24.

[6] Ibid, p.27.

[7] Ibid, p.26.

[8] However, like Billy the Kid, there are other versions of Esteban's death. One is that the Zuni people faked Esteban's death and let him live. The other story, which could be true, was that Esteban played dead and escaped. He was later captured by another tribe who was so enamored with him that they cut off his legs so that he could never escape. They also gave to him several wives that he fathered children with.

[9] Hallenbeck, *Journey of Fray Marcos*, p.33

[10] Hallenbeck, *Journey of Fray Marcos*, pp.33-34.

APPENDIX I

William Libbey's Account

From the Chicago Inter Ocean *of August 22, 1897, here is Professor William Libbey's firsthand account of his exploration of Katzimo Mesa which was touched upon in Chapter 1.*

MYTH OF THE MESA

A Daring Princeton Professor Proclaims Its Disenchantment

AZTEC MYSTERY PROBED

A Mighty Rock Ingeniously Scaled with Rope and Chair.

No Signs Upon its Top That the Red Man Ever Made It His Impregnable Home.

There is no more interesting study than that of the myths of the ancient inhabitants of this continent. Prominent among them are the stories which center around Montezuma—the Moses of the Aztecs.

The historic pueblo of Acoma is most directly connected with Montezuma and his acts, because it is said that he was born on this spot. It is true that this honor is claimed by many other pueblos, and consequently this central figure of the olden time in our southwestern territory has come to be regarded as a species of "composite photograph"—the crystallization of the characteristics of many noble men into a type which came to be regarded with veneration, and eventually deified —for he became their prophet, priest, and first ruler.

Descended from such a remote period comes the medicine man's myth, for such it turns out to be—of the former occupancy of the top of the famous Mesa Encantada, which stands about three miles north of the present site of the pueblo of Acoma.

Montezuma taught them the arts and manufactures which distinguish these tribes from their nomadic brethren of the plains, he gave them the primitive religious ideas which even today exercise a certain influence over their lives, in spite of the Christian ideas which have slowly been introduced among them by the devoted men and women who have passed their lives at these isolated posts of duty and privilege. He told them that a race of conquerors and oppressors would subdue them after he had disappeared, and he planted a tree, which they were to watch while they cared for the sacred fire which he started. When the tree fell deliverance from their enemies should come from the East, and that would be the beginning of an era of plenty, abundant rains, and prosperity. Strangely enough the fall of the tree was coincident with the entry of General Kearney into Santa Fe, but the remainder of the prophecy is yet unfulfilled. Many are the quaint stories which are connected with this majestic rock, and have come down to us through the medicine men of this once famous tribe. That they drew upon their imaginations sometimes is scarcely to be doubted, and it seems a pity that any of the supports for these fables should be removed, or that, these picturesque landscapes should be robbed of some of their delightful interest simply for the sake of verifying or disproving the possibility of the myth. It would seem better to accept the tradition and leave the mysterious wreath still twined about the altar, where it was left by almost reverent hands.

Human curiosity, however, and scientific inquisitiveness can only be tempted up to a certain point. The ghost of the Brocken has been long since dissolved into much thinner mist than ghosts are usually composed of, and the shriek of the railroad whistle as a locomotive dashes into the tunnel under the Lorelei rock has driven the fairies forever from one of their favorite haunts.

Vanishing Myths So it was that the fable of the "enchanted mesa," when its turn came, after many futile attempts had been made to solve it, turned to ashes in our hands during the past summer, and its spirit, which has so long hung over this, its unique abode, was banished by the profane touch of flesh and blood, and drifted away in the changing lights of a magnificent Western sunset glow. Not that we robbed it of any of its glory or impressiveness as a natural object of wonder, but that the veil of mystery in which it has been so long enshrined has been pulled aside and the lonely rock looks bare and forsaken, except when, under the magic influence of the moon, the fantastic rocks upon its surface seem to take shape, and its old glories live again; or when the storm clouds wreath its solemn head, and the vivid lightning dashes from the dark masses which seem to rest on its supporting surface, and light up with their lurid glare the stern, cold face of the rock; then the genis of the mesa seem to have taken possession once more, and the mind peoples the rock with the stalwart forms and blanket covered figures which today are seen in all these pueblo towns. For the life of today with its customs and habits is but a continuation of the past, and it is easy, after reading the stories of Cabeza de Vaca, Coronado, or Castenada, written more than 800 years ago, when one of these pueblos is visited, to imagine that you are looking at a bit of the past, so true are they to their traditions.

The rock itself is an interesting geological feature of the valley. In the remote past this whole depression leading to the north was covered with a mass of sedimentary rock, laid down at different times and of differing material. After deposition was complete and erosion started, this rock, as well as many others in the valley, either presented a harder material to the denuding forces than that found about them, or they occupied favored and protected positions with reference to the currents which were the active agents in the work.

The Cliff on the Plains At present its base line is a nearly level plain with an elevation of 6,200 feet above the sea level—in horizontal bands the strata rise one above the other until a height of 500 feet more is reached. Around the foot of the main cliff there is a huge heap of bowlders of all sizes, which lead upward toward its base. The height of this *pile'varies* from fifty to 150 feet and is not the least curious feature of the mass.

There are some other items worthy of note concerning the main cliff. In its eastern face some 250 feet from the bottom, there is a cave-like opening, which has been thought by some to form a passageway to the top of the rock. No trace of such opening was found on the surface, and it therefore doubtless is due to atmospheric causes, acting upon a weak spot in the structure of the rock. On the western face there is a deep circular opening like an amphitheater, which nearly divides the main rock into two portions; in fact, where the two lines meet there is a rather knifelike edge only a few inches in width, and where it is narrowest a chasm some fifty feet deep allows one to see the sky below the upper edge of the cliff to this extent. In general, the ground shape of the rock is that of a right angle triangle, the longer side of which has a deep curve in it. The flat end of this triangular mass faces the north, and the long, rather narrow point at the other end faces toward the present rock of Acoma at the south.

The Enchantment Legend The old story of its enchantment is briefly outlined. Before the advent of the whites— so say the medicine men—the fearless warriors of Acoma had built upon this impregnable rock the homes of their tribe. They were a quiet, peace-loving race, and while they tilled the fields of their fertile valley, or watched their numerous herds, they chose such sites for their adobe houses because of the security thus obtained for their wives and children and their stores. The arts and manufactures had progressed with them as with their related kinsfolk to the east and west along the tributaries of the great Pecos valley. The clay of the valley had given them the means of making the various household utensils of which they stood in need, as well as furnishing them with the sun-baked bricks of which their houses were constructed, and the cement with which the walls were built. Their herds of sheep produced the wool from which their garments and blankets were made. All was peace and prosperity until one day, when almost all of the inhabitants were away from their rock castle, a violent storm uprooted the long slab-like stone upon which their zigzag pathway to the top had been hewn. On their return from the fields they saw with consternation that they were cut off from all access to their homes and storehouses, and that they should be forced to commence anew upon some other spot. To the south of where they were, lay a great square topped rock, to which they retired, and there was built the pueblo known as Acoma. From that time to this no human foot has crossed the top of the "rock of spirits," or Kutsema, as they call it. The medicine men have told the story of the past around their council fires, and these stories have doubtless grown with the years. Many longing glances must have been cast toward that summit, and though the Indians claim that it has been visited, and made such claims this summer, when asked for the trail, or even any evidence of it, or for some idea of the character of the top, they either would not or could not tell anything about it.

An Air Line to the Mesa The idea occurred to me about three years ago that by utilizing the apparatus of the life saving service a shot line might be carried over the top of the mesa at its narrowest point, and then stouter lines or ropes hauled over until one could be put in position that was strong enough to stand the strain of its own weight, plus that of a man together with the frictional strain produced by his weight passing over the line. I found that I could obtain the co-operation of the life saving service and all my plans were perfected in the fall of 1895. They were interfered with at that time, and since then no favorable opportunity presented itself until this summer.

I had examined many other devices for carrying a line over the rock, but became satisfied that the plan as outlined above, was the only practical one, in view of the climatic conditions of the place. There was, for example, either too much or too little wind for devices which depended upon that element for support during the period of our stay near the Mesa. In view of the result obtained we have every reason to be satisfied with the methods.

Mr. Bridgman and I left New York about the middle of July, and our ton of baggage provoked amusing comment on the part of the railroad men at least. About one-half of it consisted of coils of rope, and I doubt whether any such "outfit" was ever put together before. The faking boxes and the cannon each came in for their share of curious comment, and many were the dubious headshakes and suppressed jokes upon the latest idea of the "tenderfoot" outfit. The faking boxes were conundrums that were invariably "given up" by all hands.

Moving Upon the Mystery We had obtained most of our camping equipment and stores through the courtesy of the authorities at Fort Wingate, where a delightful day was spent, and were off for the Mesa early on the morning of July 19. We had been materially aided in our preparations by the kind services of Mr. Marmon, at Laguna, at whose hospitable house we had spent several days. Our party was now increased by the addition of Gordon D. Pearce and a cook. All our effects were loaded upon two large wagons, and three of us, with the idea of making the loads lighter for the teams, started ahead to walk, thinking that they would overtake us when the level roads of the Acoma valley were reached. Evening came, and the teams were nowhere in sight, and we were still walking. We passed by and gazed upon the Mesa with some wonder and considerable more reverence than we had previously felt for it and saw Acoma rock was but three miles distant, we decided to push on and take our chances for bed and supper there, rather than wait for our belated companions on the wagons. It was well we did so, for we were well treated, and the supper touched a sympathetic chord, after that long walk of about twenty-six miles without dinner and with but one drink of water from a rainwater tank, which would not have been very inviting had it not been wet. We enjoyed our new and strange surroundings to the full, and with bed and breakfast secure felt rich, as we promenaded the top of this historic rock quite as much to the enjoyment of the natives as we in turn took in them. We watched for signs of our companions as the last rays of the setting sun gleamed across the valley, but in vain. We were, however, more than repaid for our trouble and pains by the wonderful views of the Mesa and the surrounding valley as obtained from this vantage ground.

At the Foot of the Rock The next morning, after a substantial meal, we saw a campfire just at the foot of the Mesa, and knew that our party had arrived. After an hour's walk we rejoined them. Then a preliminary search was made for a camp. One available water tank, about half a mile east of the Mesa, was all that offered itself, and a location was chosen near this spot. Here the tents and camp stores were deposited, and the rest of my equipment, after a careful study of the face of the cliff had been made, were taken to a point near the southern end of the rock, which seemed best fitted for our attack. The rest of the day was taken up in fitting up the camp, and then our teams departed for Laguna. We were joined the next day by Mr. Knapp, who had been interested in the enterprise and asked to be allowed to watch the proceedings. He and his pony proved valuable allies during the next few days.

On Wednesday morning the shot line was faked, by running it around the series of tall pegs fastened in the edge of the bottom of the box, which had been removed from the box. The line passed diagonally across the board from one pin to another until one layer had been put in position, then the next layer was run on in such a manner that it laid at right angles to the one below it, and so on until all the 1,500 feet had been coiled up. Then the top and sides of the box were placed over them and fastened down. The whole box was then turned upside down, the bottom board unloosened and removed with its pins. This resulted in leaving the rope coiled in the box in such a condition that one layer would be removed at a time, and the whole taken from the box without producing one tremendous snarl. The whole was as free as a bundle of snowflakes.

Shooting a Line The two and one-half inch Lyle gun was then unpacked and mounted. Meanwhile the end of the shot line bad been soaking in a pail of water, to prevent, if possible, its being burnt off by the powder upon the discharge of the gun. The shot was a long, cylindrical mass of iron weighing twenty-five pounds; both ends were conical, but one was prolonged by a cast steel shaft of six inches in length. In the end of which was a circular, opening through which the cord passed when it was fastened to the bolt. Four ounces of powder in a little flannel bag were placed in the gun, the shot poshed upon it, and then as the primer was inserted everybody was warned away from behind the gun. The lanyard was pulled, a thunderous echo resounded from the cliff, and all eyes followed the shot as it turned over in its flight and then sped toward the cliff. Alas, it was only toward the cliff, the angle of elevation, forty degrees, though apparently ample, had not been enough to carry the shot clear of the top. It struck about 100 feet below the top, burst into two pieces, and, leaving a great scar on the face of the rock. Its parts fell into the rubbish heap at the base of the cliff, where they were afterward found. The shotline was hauled back after considerable trouble with coils about bushes and rocks, which were peculiarly perverse. It was faked again, and at 11:30 all was ready for a second shot. The roar of the little cannon was once more heard, the line rattled along merrily out of the box, and this time, to our delight, clear sky was seen between the shot and the top of the rock. The shot reached its greatest height, almost directly over the Mesa, and in the downward flight came close to the other side of the rock. Finally the cord stopped leaving the box, and we knew from the fact that very little was left in the box that it must be very near the bottom, opposite to us, for an angular measurement had given the height of the cliff at about 500 feet. We went to the other side, recovered the shot which had done such good work for us, made the line fast to a rock on that side, and went to dinner, well satisfied with our work, for we knew that the first step had been successfully taken toward the mastery of the Mesa.

Placing the Main Rope The next two days were devoted to the hauling of successively heavier ropes over the top of the Mesa. The first lines were hauled over by hand. The half-inch rope required a horse, and the inch rope proved too much for both horse and men together. Fortunately for us, just at the time when we were called to a halt in this way, Padre Martin drove past on his meandering path over his 26,000 square mile parish, and politely gave us the use of his team, and the main line was soon in place.

Before this heavy rope was pulled up I had spliced a block in it securely at a point 750 feet from the end, which was to remain on the eastern side of the Mesa. I had already ascertained by means of one of the other lines that the distance between the edge of the cliff and a large bowlder near us, and to which we proposed to anchor the rope, was 700 feet, approximately. Through this block a leading line was passed, by means of which the half-inch rope or whip line was afterward hauled through the block. While the main line and block, with its leading line, was being hauled up, I watched the progress of the block, with my pistol in hand. Mr. Pearce had been stationed at the southern end of the Mesa with another pistol, at a point where he could hear my shot, and at the same time see the team, and where the driver could hear the report of the pistol. This was to be the signal that the block had reached its position directly on the edge of the cliff. The plan worked to perfection, and no difficulty was afterward experienced in passing the half-inch rope through the block. The traveling block was then passed over the main rope, and one hand of the whip line attached to it. The other end of the whip line was led through a block secured to a cedar tree, stuck up in such a position that when the horses were attached to this end of the line they could be driven along a comparatively level bit of the plain, and in full view of the cliff, so that the driver could see for himself and hear all the directions given very plainly. All our appliances were in order by Friday noon, and we went to dinner with the anticipation of some exhilarating work in the afternoon.

Up Goes the Professor When we came back to our base of operation the boatswain's chair, consisting of a board from the cover of one of our boxes, was fastened to the ring of the traveling block. A large rock was placed on it, and the order to "hoist away" was given. All moved very properly, and after the rock had been safely returned to us, I tied myself to the chair and lashed my camera and tripod to the ropes. My other instruments, such as barometer, etc., were stowed away in my pockets. After asking who was to be the next traveler to follow me and noticing that the desire to see the top of that rock had perceptibly diminished, I was glad to find that one of the party was willing to trust the cobweb we had constructed after I had tested it myself. Then came the moment for which I had waited for many days. Under the guidance of "John," our faithful Indian teamster, the horse and his little mate moved off. The man would be a block. Indeed, who could not experience the thrill of such a situation. Fear was not a part of it, for I knew that the main rope upon which my life depended was six times stronger than I needed. I had put those splices in myself, and put them in to stay. I knew the rope had not been frayed perceptibly, and best of all, I knew that in my companions below I had a set of serious and steady sheet anchors, endowed with large amounts of common sence [sic], which I felt sure would be applied instantly and properly, with nerves steady at least with the solid ground beneath them. A man can do a lot of skyrocketing with such backing. Up we went for nearly three minutes. I had found out that the speaking trumpet was a wholly useless member of the company, for the wall of reeks sent my words down below with perfect clearness, and no effort was necessary on my part to make my directions understood, even when at the top.

At last the edge of the cliff was reached. I found that if I had picked out the landing place I could not have chosen a better one than that across which the shot had carried the first cord. A gently arched surface along which the rope curved thus distributed the strain over a larger area, and prevented its being concentrated on a single cross section of the rope, on a sharp edge, was the first item I noted, and which increased my confidence in the strength of the contrivance.

The Summit Reached After disengaging my camera and the rest of my appliances and placing them on the rock above me, I stood up in the chair, and, swinging my leg over the main rope, scrambled up beside them, to be greeted by a series of characteristic plaudits from below. The chair was hauled back, and in the meantime I had started on an investigation of the top of the rock, for I was not sure that I had succeeded even then in reaching the main summit. A chasm which seemed to cut the rock from some distance down from the top bad been a disturbing element in my thoughts. After some scrambling over the very broken, surface of the rock I found, to my dismay, that the great amphitheater on the west side had approached the eastern cliff line as closely that a mere knife edge was all that was left in some places and that directly below the edge upon which I stood was a chasm clear through the rock from one side to the other of a depth of some fifty or sixty feet, on either side of which for 350 feet downward the view was uninterrupted to the rocks below. Truly an interesting situation. Fortunately, below my position, at a depth of ten or twelve feet, there was a narrow projection of the rock six or seven inches wide and nearly twice as long, directly opposite to which was a knob of rock about two feet square. If this could be reached the question was solved. I quickly determined that it could be done if a ladder could be obtained from Acoma, and so informed my companions below. Mr. Pearce was then hoisted up to my airy position, and while the team was away after the ladder we had ample time to explore to our complete satisfaction the portion of the rock of which we now had possession, in spite of the protests of a few ravens. He assured me that his sensations on the way up had been many and various, but in the same breath, also stated that he would not have missed the unique experience for the world.

Triumphant but Disappointed By 6 o'clock the ladder arrived, and was hauled up to us. Securing it in place by means of a rope passed around the top of a rock, I descended it, and, balancing myself, jumped across the four feet intervening and landed safely on the perch on the opposite side. This bit of gymnastics was much more of a nerve test for my companion than coming up the rope, so I had to pursue my investigations on the main rock by myself. For two hours I walked over the surface of the rock, which is much larger than the portion first visited, covering some ten or twelve acres. It is a splendid site for a pueblo. If some means of access could be devised, but it could not have been freer of all traces of former occupation if it had been thoroughly swept up the day before. Only once was it that a doubt crossed my mind — when I came across a cairnlike monument, which looked as though it might have been constructed by human hands; but the possibility of its being the result of erosion is also quite as strong as the other. No bits of pottery, no broken household utensils of any sort, no traces of construction of any sort were visible, not even the deepening of the natural surface of any of the rock cavities for the purpose of rain-water storage for drinking use betrayed the slightest indication that the top of the mesa had ever been the prehistoric home of the Acomas. Sadly, as the sun was setting, I retraced my steps to the chasm, jumped across to the ladder, and was soon busy telling the story to the upturned faces below me.

We retreated in good order to camp, and the next morning in two hours' time all trace of our occupation of the summit had disappeared—except the little ladder, which was left in place for someone else to take down when the next attack is made upon the disenchanted home of Montezuma.

WILLIAM LIBBEY.

APPENDIX II

W.H. Byerts' Iron Door Mine

This is W.H. Byerts' full entry into The Mexican Mining Journal *of September, 1912 on the Iron Door Mine covered in Chapter 9.*

This famous old property which is known at present only through legend and history was one of the most productive and wealthy properties on the American continent when worked over three hundred and fifty years ago. Worked by the Spaniards with the crudest of implements and methods, millions of dollars were extracted and the property was given a world wide reputation.

As the early Spanish explorers went up the Rio Grande valley a number of properties were located and worked with very satisfactory results and tradition tells us that some of these properties were of exceptional richness and only those that produced ore that was easy to treat were touched for there was no method of handling the rebellious ores with the primitive methods of metallurgical treatment known at that time.

At what now is the site of the city of Socorro, these early times was located Mission City, which became famous for its mineral wealth and the large bodies of chloride and sulphide [sic] ores of gold and silver. The location was selected primarily because of the large spring of pure warm water which gushes out of the rock at the base of the Socorro mountains, three miles to the west of the Rio Grande river bottoms. The city was founded by catholic monks and called the Holy Mission City.

This beautiful valley with its fertile soils, producing wonderful fruits and champaign grapes soon became a vast garden, the monks importing the choicest fruits and grapes from Europe to which the soil was well adapted. While wonderful progress was being made in agriculture and horticulture, the mines in the Blue canyon, three and a half miles to the west of the Mission City were being opened up and their production was increasing yearly. The amount of gold and silver bullion that was annually exported to Europe amounted to millions of dollars and Mission City became famous through its wonderful mineral production.

These mines were worked for nearly a hundred years with an ever increasing number of men and corresponding increase in output, up to the year 1684 when calamity befell the community and the work was brought to a sudden conclusion. At this time an earthquake of unusual force broke off an overhanging ledge of mountain precipitating millions of tons of rock, completely burying the mouth of this famous property, which was then known as the "Iron Door." The mine had but one opening, through a tunnel, which was closed with a heavy iron door from which the property derived its name.

At the time of the calamity, the property was worked principally by convict labor, being made up mostly of indians, who as prisoners were forced to work out their sentences in the mines, which served as a prison as well as mine. The ores extracted were treated in the primitive adobe furnace, the ruins of which were still to be seen up to the year 1880. Besides the enormous wealth that was exported each year, the church became a treasure house in which was stored up great wealth in gold and silver. History tells us that there was connected with the church a number of silversmiths and goldsmiths, who were continuously engaged in fashioning filigrees, ornaments, images, urns and other decorations out of gold and silver for use in the church. A golden chandelier suspended from the ceiling by heavy silver chains together with the altar ornaments of gold and silver were evidence of the wealth of the mine and thrift of the people. The church was the wealthiest in the country at that time and the city was the largest and wealthiest in the southwest.

Early people had to reckon which proved their downfall and resulted in the obliteration of all that had been accomplished, namely the indians.

As these savage tribesmen saw their people being forced into the mines and their lands being taken up by the white man a spirit of restlessness began to grow upon them and finally resulted in the union of the various tribes for the purpose of wiping this new civilization out of the country and restoring to themselves their lands and property. This rebellion against the white man was declared in the latter part of August in the same year that the earthquake happened and at about the same time, the overthrow of Mission City being but a few days after the earthquake. At the time when the people were at work in an attempt to rescue the 500 imprisoned miners in the Iron Door mine, the indian hordes were coming down the river for an assault on the city and the work was abandoned leaving the hundreds of miners to perish, being entombed by thousands of tons of rock and history does not record that the property was ever relocated or opened. The white man was driven from this section of the country and south into Mexico leaving the country to the indians, who held it for over a hundred years afterwards.[1] Every vestige of this early civilization and immense wealth was wiped out; the church alone remaining, a monument to that which had gone before. All traces of the mines and city were destroyed during this time and not until the year 1880 was there another mining venture promoted.

At this time a number of claims were located including the Torrence and Merrit, Horning Star and others. The Torrence and Merrit were worked from 1880 to 1885 and produced over a million dollars worth of bullion and the deepest workings did not go down over 150 feet, only the surface deposits being worked. All of these properties have been purchased by one company together with the location where the famous Iron Door property was located and are again known as the Iron Door Mines of Socorro. At the present time a tunnel is being driven under the old workings from the base of the mountain, which will open up the mine at a depth of 500 feet. The tunnel is now in over 500 feet and is being pushed day and night with every expectation of opening up one of the great gold-silver deposits of the southwest.

Section Notes

---

[1] Byerts' dates were inaccurate across the board in this article. The Pueblo Revolt occurred in 1680, not 1684 as he remembered it. But the most glaring error was in the statement that the Spaniards didn't reconquer New Spain for another hundred years. The indigenous peoples only reclaimed their lands for about a decade before the Spanish returned in the early 1690s.

APPENDIX III

Coronado's Report to Viceroy Mendoza, Part IV

The following is Francisco Vázquez de Coronado's Report to Viceroy Mendoza, Part IV, compiled and delivered in the year 1540, which more or less retconned the reports of Fray Marcos de Niza:

These Indians say that the kingdom of Totonteac, which the father provincial praised so much, saying that it was something marvelous, and of such a very great size, & that cloth was made there, is a hot lake, on the edge of which there are five or six houses. There used to be some others, but these have been destroyed by war. The kingdom of Marata can not be found, nor do these Indians know anything about it. The kingdom of Acus is a single small city, where they raise cotton, and this is called Acucu. I say that this is the country, because Acus, with or without the aspiration, is not a word in this region; & because it seems to me that Acucu may be derived from Acus, I say that it is this town which has been converted into the kingdom of Acus. They tell me that there are some other small ones not far from this settlement, which are situated on a river which I have seen and of which the Indians have told me. God knows that I wish I had better news to write to Your Lordship, but I must give you the truth, and, as I wrote you from Culuacan, I must advise you of the good as well as of the bad. But you may be assured that if there had been all the riches and treasures of the world, I could not have done more in His Majesty's service and in that of Your Lordship than I have done, in coming here where you commanded me to go, carrying, both my companions & myself, our food on our backs for 300 leagues, and traveling on foot many days, making our way over hills and rough mountains, besides other labors which I refrain from mentioning. Nor do I think of stopping until my death, if it serves His Majesty or Your Lordship to have it so.

Three days after I captured this city, some of the Indians who lived here came to offer to make peace. They brought me some turquoises and poor mantles, and I received them in His Majesty's name with as good a speech as I could, making them understand the purpose of my coming to this country, which is, in the name of His Majesty and by the commands of Your Lordship, that they and all others in this province should become Christians and should know the true God for their Lord, and His Majesty for their king and earthly lord. After this they returned to their houses and suddenly, the next day, they packed up their goods and property, their women and children, & fled to the hills, leaving their towns deserted, with only some few remaining in them. Seeing this, I went to the town which I said was larger than this, eight or ten days later, when I had recovered from my wounds. I found a few of them there, whom I told that they ought not to feel any fear, and I asked them to summon their lord to me. By what I can find out or observe, however, none of these towns have any, since I have not seen any principal house by which any superiority over others could be shown. Afterward, an old man, who said he was their lord, came with a mantle made of many pieces, with whom I argued as long as he stayed with me. He said that he would come to see me with the rest of the chiefs of the country, three days later, in order to arrange the relations which should exist between us. He did so, and they brought me some little ragged mantles and some turquoises. I said that they ought to come down from their strongholds and return to their houses with their wives and children, and that they should become Christians, and recognize His Majesty as their king and lord. But they still remain in their strongholds, with their wives and all their property.

I commanded them to have a cloth painted for me, with all the animals that they know in that country, and although they are poor painters, they quickly painted two for me, one of the animals and the other of the birds and fishes. They say that they will bring their children so that our priests may instruct them, & that they desire to know our law. They declare that it was foretold among them more than fifty years ago that a people such as we are should come, and the direction they should come from, and that the whole country would be conquered. So far as I can find out, the water is what these Indians worship, because they say that it makes the corn grow and sustains their life, and that the only other reason they know is because their ancestors did so. I have tried in every way to find out from the natives of these settlements whether they know of any other peoples or provinces or cities. They tell me about seven cities which are at a considerable distance, which are like these, except that the houses there are not like these, but are made of earth, and small, and that they raise much cotton there. The first of these four places about which they know is called, they say, Tucano. They could not tell me much about the others. I do not believe that they tell me the truth, because they think that I shall soon have to depart from them and return home. But they will quickly find that they are deceived in this. I sent Don Pedro de Tobar there, with his company & some other horsemen, to see it. I would not have dispatched this packet to Your Lordship until I had learned what he found there, if I thought that I should have any news from him within twelve or fifteen days. However, as he will remain away at least thirty, and, considering that this information is of little importance and that the cold and the rains are approaching, it seemed to me that I ought to do as Your Lordship commanded me in your instructions, which is, that as soon as I arrived here, I should advise you thereof, ad this I do, by sending you the plain narrative of what I have seen, which is bad enough, as you may perceive. I have determined to send throughout all the surrounding regions, in order to find out whether there is anything, and to suffer every extremity before I give up this enterprise, and to serve His Majesty, if I can find any way in which to do it, and not to lack in diligence until Your Lordship directs me as to what I ought to do.

We have great need of pasture, and you should know, also, that among all those who are here there is not one pound of raisins, nor sugar, nor oil, nor wine, except barely half a quart, which is saved to say mass, since everything is consumed, and part was lost on the way. Now, you can provide us with what appears best; but if you are thinking of sending us cattle, you should know that it will be necessary for them to spend at least a year on the road, because they can not come in any other way, nor any quicker. I would have liked to send to Your Lordship, with this dispatch, many samples of the things which they have in this country, but the trip is so long & rough that it is difficult for me to do so. However, I send you twelve small mantles, such as the people of this country ordinarily wear, and a garment which seems to me to be very well made. I kept it because it seemed to me to be of very good workmanship, and because I do not think that anyone else has ever seen in these Indies any work done with a needle, unless it were done since the Spaniards settled here. And I also send two cloths painted with the animals which they have in this country, although, as I said, the painting is very poorly done, because the artist did not spend more than one day in painting it. I have seen other paintings of the walls of these houses which have much better proportion and are done much better.

I send you a cow skin, some turquoises, and two earrings of the same, and fifteen of the Indian combs, and some plates decorated with these turquoises, and two baskets made of wicker, of which the Indians have a large supply. I also send two rolls, such as the women usually wear on their heads when they bring water from the spring, the same way that they do in Spain. One of these Indian women, with one of these rolls on her head, will carry a jar of water up a ladder without touching it with her hands. And, lastly, I send you samples of the weapons with which the natives of this country fight, a shield, a hammer, and a bow with some arrows, among which there are two with bone points, the like of which have never been seen, according to what these conquerors say. As far as I can judge, it does not appear to me that there is any hope of getting gold or silver, but I trust in God that, if there is any, we shall get our share of it, and it shall not escape us through any lack of diligence in the search. I am unable to give Your Lordship any certain information about the dress of the women, because the Indians keep them guarded so carefully that I have not seen any, except two old women. These had on two long skirts reaching down to their feet and open in front, & a girdle, & they are tied together with some cotton strings. I asked the Indians to give me one of those which they wore, to send to you, since they were not willing to show me the women. They brought me two mantles, which are these that I send, almost painted over. They have two tassels, like the women of Spain, which hang somewhat over their shoulders.

The death of the negro [Esteban de Dorantes] is perfectly certain, because many of the things which he wore have been found, and the Indians say that they killed him here because the Indians of Chichilticale said that he was a bad man, and not like the Christians, because the Christians never kill women, and he killed them, and because he assaulted their women, whom the Indians love better then themselves. Therefore they determined to kill him, but they did not do it in the way that was reported, because they did not kill any of the others who came with him, nor did they kill the lad from the province of Petatlan, who was with him, but they took him and kept him in safe custody until now. When I tried to secure him, they made excuses for not giving him to me, for two or three days, saying that he was dead, and at other ties that the Indians of Acucu had taken him away. But when I finally told them that I should be very angry if they did not give him to me, they gave him to me. He is an interpreter; for although he cannot talk much, he understands very well.

Some gold & silver has been found in this place, which those who know about minerals say is not bad. I have not yet been able to learn from these people where they got it. I perceive that they refuse to tell me the truth in everything, because they think that I shall have to depart from here in a short time, as I have said. But I trust in God that they will not be able to avoid answering much longer. I beg Your Lordship to make a report of the success of this expedition to His Majesty, because there is nothing more than what I have already said. I shall not do so until it shall please God to grant that we find what we desire. Our Lord God protect and keep your most illustrious Lordship. From the province of Cevola, and this city of Granada, the 3d of August, 1540. Francisco Vazquez de Coronado kisses the hand of your most illustrious Lordship.

BIBLIOGRAPHY

Books

Aragón, Ray John de. *Enchanted Legends and Lore of New Mexico: Witches, Ghosts & Spirits*. The History Press, 2012.

Bancroft, Hubert Howe. *History of Arizona and New Mexico, 1530-1888*. Harvard University, 1889.

Bullock, Alice. *Monumental Ghosts*. Sunstone Press, 2016.

Charles, Beula. *Tales of the Tularosa*. By the author, 1959.

Childress, David Hatcher. *Lost Cities and Ancient Mysteries of the Southwest*. Adventures Unlimited Press, 2009.

Cozzens, Gary. *Tres Ritos: A History of Three Rivers, New Mexico*. The History Press, 2015.

Dornan, Ellen. *Forgotten Tales of New Mexico*. The History Press, 2012.

Ebright, Malcolm & Rick Hendricks. *The Witches of Abiquiu: The Governor, the Priest, the Genízaro Indians, and the Devil*. University of New Mexico Press, 2006.

García, Nasario. *Tales of Witchcraft and the Supernatural in the Pecos Valley*. Western Edge Press, 1999.

Gregg, Josiah. *Commerce of the Prairies*. University of Oklahoma Press, 1958.

Hallenbeck, Cleve. *The Journey of Fray Marcos*. Southern Methodist University Press, 1987.

Horgan, Paul. *Conquistadors in North American History*. Farrar, Straus & Company, 1963.

Hudnall, Ken & Sharon. *Spirits of the Border IV: The History and Mystery of New Mexico*. Omega Press, 2005.

Kutz, Jack. *Mysteries and Miracles of New Mexico*. Rhombus Press, 1988.

-------------- *More Mysteries and Miracles of New Mexico*. Rhombus Publishing Company, 1998.

L'Amour, Louis. Louis L'Amour's Lost Treasures: *The Haunted Mesa*. Bantam Books, 2019.

Lummis, Charles. *A New Mexico David: And Other Stories and Sketches of the Southwest*. Charles Scribner's Sons, 1891.

McKenna, James A. *Black Range Tales*. The Rio Grande Press, 1936/1984.

Meadows, John P. and John P. Wilson, Ed. *Pat Garrett and Billy the Kid as I Knew Them*. University of New Mexico Press, 2004.

Porter, Clyde and Mae Reed (Compilers) and John E. Sunder (Editor). *Matt Field on the Santa Fe Trail*. University of Oklahoma Press, 1960.

Robinson, Sherry. *Apache Voices: Their Stories of Survival as Told to Eve Ball*. University of New Mexico Press, 2000.

Articles

Galbraith, Den. "Iron Door Mine of Blue Canyon." *Frontier Times* (Sep/Oct 1964).

Hesse, Wally. "Capitan's Gold." *Treasure Search*, n.d.

Howe, Carl. "Did the Dutchman find Montezuma's Treasure?" *Gold!* (Almanac, 1969).

INDEX

ABOUT THE AUTHOR

John LeMay was born and raised in Roswell, NM, the "UFO Capital of the World." He is the author of over 50 books, many of them on the history of the Southwest such as *Tall Tales and Half Truths of Billy the Kid*, and *Roswell USA: Towns That Celebrate UFOs, Lake Monsters, Bigfoot and Other Weirdness*. In addition to non-fiction, he is also the author of the novels *The Noted Desperado Pancho Dumez* and *Once Upon a Time in Fort Sumner*. He is also the editor/publisher of *Strange West Magazine* and has written for Western journals and magazines such as *True West*, *The Coalition Journal*, the *Tombstone Epitaph*, and the *Wild West History Association Journal*. He is a Past President of the Board of Directors for the Historical Society for Southeast New Mexico.

The following titles are available for purchase on Amazon.com, and are available to bookstores at a wholesale discount via Ingram Content Group (ISBNs of available editions listed for this purpose)

CRYPTOZOOLOGY/COWBOYS & SAURIANS

Cowboys & Saurians: Prehistoric Beasts as Seen by the Pioneers explores dinosaur sightings from the pioneer period via real newspaper reports from the time. Well-known cases like the Tombstone Thunderbird are covered along with more obscure cases like the Crosswicks Monster and more. Softcover (357 pp/5.06" X 7.8") Suggested Retail: $19.95 ISBN: 978-1-7341546-1-0

Cowboys & Saurians: Ice Age zeroes in on snowbound saurians like the Cerato-saurus of the Arctic Circle and a Tyrannosaurus of the Tundra, as well as sightings of Ice Age megafauna like mammoths, glyptodonts, Sarkastodons and Saber-toothed tigers. Tales of a land that time forgot in the Arctic are also covered. Softcover (264 pp/5.06" X 7.8") Suggested Retail: $14.99 ISBN: 978-1-7341546-7-2

Southerners & Saurians takes the series formula of exploring newspaper accounts of monsters in the pioneer period with an eye to the Old South. In addition to dinosaurs are covered Lizardmen, Frogmen, giant leeches and mosquitoes, and the Dingocroc, which might be an alien rather than a prehistoric survivor. Softcover (202 pp/5.06" X 7.8") Suggested Retail: $13.99 ISBN: 978-1-7344730-4-9

Cowboys & Saurians South of the Border explores the saurians of Central and South America, like the Patagonian Plesiosaurus that was really an lemisch, plus tales of the Neo-Mylodon, a menacing monster from underground called the Minhocao, Glyptodonts, and even Bolivia's three-headed dinosaur! Softcover (412 pp/ 5.06"X7.8") Suggested Retail: $17.95 ISBN: 978-1-953221-73-5

UFOLOGY/THE REAL COWBOYS & ALIENS IN CONJUNCTION WITH ROSWELL BOOKS

The Real Cowboys and Aliens: Early American UFOs explores UFO sightings in the USA between the years 1800-1864. Stories of encounters sometimes involved famous figures in U.S. history such as Lewis and Clark, and Thomas Jefferson.Hardcover (242pp/6" X 9") Softcover (262 pp/5.06" X 7.8") Suggested Retail: $24.99 (hc)/$15.95(sc) ISBN: 978-1-7341546-8-9\(hc)/978-1-7344730-8-7(sc)

The second entry in the series, *Old West UFOs*, covers reports spanning the years 1865-1895. Includes tales of Men in Black, Reptilians, Spring-Heeled Jack, Sasquatch from space, and other alien beings, in addition to the UFOs and airships. Hardcover (276 pp/6" X 9") Softcover (308 pp/5.06" X 7.8") Suggested Retail: $29.95 (hc)/$17.95(sc) ISBN: 978-1-7344730-0-1 (hc)/ 978-1-73447 30-2-5 (sc)

The third entry in the series, *The Coming of the Airships*, encompasses a short time frame with an incredibly high concentration of airship sightings between 1896-1899. The famous Aurora, Texas, UFO crash of 1897 is covered in depth along with many others. Hardcover (196 pp/6" X 9") Softcover (222 pp/5.06" X 7.8") Suggested Retail: $24.99 (hc)/$15.95(sc) ISBN: 978-1-7347816 -1-8 (hc)/978-1-7347816-0-1(sc)

Featuring cases the authors missed, *The Lost Cases* covers things such as the skyquakes recorded by Lewis and Clark, airships and the Spanish American War, Pancho Villa and crystal skulls, lost alien tribe of the Tundra, invisible alien monsters, the Great Moon Hoax of 1835, hellhounds and airships, the Sonora Airship Club and more. Softcover (252 pp/5.06" X 7.8") Suggested Retail: $18.99 ISBN: 978-1-953221-55-1

COWBOYS & SAURIANS CONT'D

Cowboys & Saurians: Dinosaurs Down Under takes the series to Australia to explore tales of the cattle devouring Burrunjor, the dreaded Diprotodon, the terrible Tantanoola Tiger, the marsupial Sasquatch known as the Yowie, plus Thylacines, Bunyips, giant rabbits, Megalodons and dinosaurs in nearby New Zealand. Softcover (240 pp/ 5.06" X 7.8") Suggested Retail: $14.95 ISBN: 978-1-953221-34-6

As the title suggest, *Cowboys & Saurians in the Modern Era* takes the series into the 20th Century with tales of the Texas Pterosaur flap of 1976, the Bladenboro Beast of the 1950s, the Busco Turtle Beast of the 1940s, dinosaur sightings in the Great Depression and far out tales of mini-mastodons, dinosaur men, and Snallygasters. Softcover (320 pp/ 5.06" X 7.8") Suggested Retail: $19.95 ISBN: 978-1-953221-22-3

Settlers & Serpents wrangles the best "Snaik Stories" of the Southwest and beyond in a single volume. Whether it's simple giant snakes or lake serpents, they're corralled in the pages within. Also included are entries on the Leviathan in Mesoamerica and the Southwest plus a detailed look at the giant rattlesnake of Pecos Pueblo. Softcover (180 pp/ 5.06" X 7.8") Suggested Retail: $14.99 ISBN: 978-1-953221-21-6

Written for young readers ages 9-12, *Monsters of the Old South* collects the best creature stories of the swamplands including the White River Monster, Green Eyes, the Crocodingo, the Averasboro Gallinipper, the Tennessee Snake Woman, the Arkansas Gowrow, Bigfoot in the Mississippi River and more. Softcover (122 pp/4.25" X 7") Suggested Retail: $12.99 ISBN: 978-17347816-9-4

THE REAL COWBOYS & ALIENS CONT'D

Early 20th Century UFOs kicks off a new series that investigates UFO sightings of the early 1900s. Includes tales of UFOs sighted over the *Titanic* as it sunk, Nikola Tesla receiving messages from the stars, an alien being found encased in ice, and a possible virus from outer space!Hardcover (196 pp/6" X 9") Softcover (222 pp/5.06" X 7.8") Suggested Retail: $27.99 (hc)/$16.95(sc) ISBN: 978-1-7347816-1-8 (hc)/978-1-73478 16-0-1(sc)

UFOs in the Roaring Twenties takes a look at UFO sightings in the 1920s just as the title suggests, along with accounts of Mothman in Nebraska, Lincoln LaPaz's first UFO case, Men in Black investigating an airship crash in Braxton County, West Virginia, Camden's Cosmic Sniper, and much more! Softcover (248 pp/5.06" X 7.8") Suggested Retail: $19.99 ISBN: 978-1-953221-51-3

UFOs of the Turbulent Thirties concludes the authors' investigation of the last unexplored decade of Ufology in the Great Depression with accounts of Mothman, Ghost Fliers, Nazi Bells, the Underground City of the Lizard People, a vanished village on the tundra, and even gangsters and aliens. Softcover (212 pp/5.06" X 7.8") Suggested Retail: $17.95 ISBN: 978-1-953221-35-3

Written for young readers ages 9-12, *Space Monsters of the Old West* collects the best alien sightings of the Wild West including Mummies from Mars, Bigfoot from the Moon, Pascagoula's space ghouls, the Crawfordsville Monster, Spring-Heeled Jack, Blobs from space, and even the dinosaurian alien Meter, Iowa. Softcover (120 pp/4.25" X 7") Suggested Retail: $12.99 ISBN: 978-1-953221-87-2

COWBOYS & MONSTERS

Cowboys & Monsters features potentially true stories of real vampires, werewolves, and even mummies unique to America's Wild West period. Examples include the cursed mummy of John Wilkes Booth, New Orleans immortal vampire Jacques St. Germain, precursors to the Beast of Bray Road, and the origins of Skinwalker Ranch. Softcover (316 pp/5.06" X 7.8") Suggested Retail: $19.99 ISBN: 978-1-953221-46-9

The first entry in this trilogy of non-fiction terror sinks its teeth into the lore of the vampire in North America and Mexico, with detailed rundowns on the vampire hunters of Exeter, Rhode Island, a tribe of Bat People, the nocturnal shape-shifting vampire witches of Tlaxcala, the immortal ways of Comte St. Germain in New Orleans and more. Softcover (200 pp/ 5.06" X 7.8") Suggested Retail: $12.99 ISBN: 978-1-953221-38-4

Mummies of the Americas explores Death Valley's city of the Dead, King Tut's Tomb along the Arkansas, the Egyptian City of the Grand Canyon plus the famous mummies of John Wilkes Boothe, Elmer McCurdy, the Cardiff Giant, the Mummy of Helldorado, and even Billy the Kid's pickled trigger finger! Softcover (200 pp/5.06" X 7.8") Suggested Retail: $12.99 ISBN: 978-1-953221-37-7

Cowboys & Dogmen is devoted to tales of werewolves of the Wild West including the dreaded Navajo skinwalker, the Watrous Werewolf, the Beast of the Land Between Lakes, the Hellhounds of El Dorado Canyon, the dreaded Dog Eater, the Wahhoo, the Wolf Man of Versailles, the Michigan Dog-Man and more! Softcover (212 pp/5.06" X 7.8") Suggested Retail: $12.99 ISBN: 978-1-953221-36-0

FICTION/ MISC. HISTORY

The first novel from historian John LeMay weaves a fantastic web of fiction via real life mysteries and legends of New Mexico, namely the puzzling theft and return of Billy the Kid's tombstone in 1976, the legend of the Lost Adams Diggings, the villainous Santa Fe Ring, and the enigmatic Acoma Mesa. Softcover (250 pp/5.5" X 7.5") Suggested Retail: $14.95 ISBN: 978-1-953221-42-1

The year is 1950, and old timers connected to the long-dead outlaw Billy the Kid are turning up murdered in New Mexico. Some blame the killings on the avenging witch of the Navajo nation, the skinwalker, while others think it's no coincidence that a man claiming to be a surviving Billy the Kid is set to meet with the governor soon... Softcover (260 pp/5.5" X 7.5") Suggested Retail: $16.95 ISBN: 978-1-953221-32-2

Roswell, USA, the long-forgotten debut work of John LeMay, is available again and covers the minutia of the infamous Roswell UFO Crash of 1947. Notable chapters include tales of an alien ghost haunting the old airbase, monsters in the nearby Bottomless Lakes, and even a dinosaur sighting outside of town. Softcover (248 pp/6" X 9") Suggested Retail: $14.95 ISBN: 978-0-9817597-5-3

This biography, for the first time ever, tells the history of western journalist Ash Upson, who ghostwrote Pat Garrett's *The Authentic Life of Billy the Kid* in 1882 and also reproduces many of Upson's letters that detailed the harsh realities of frontier life in New Mexico during the turbulent Lincoln County War. Softcover (318 pp/5.5" X 8.5") Suggested Retail: $16.99 ISBN: 978-1953221919